This book is dedicated to th
as it was being written; M.F
My gratitude goes out to ah
come during visitation days. Your continued love and support kept me going and served as a lighthouse during stormy weather.

Special thanks and appreciation to my father, the Keating family, the Jones-Parra family, my cousin Ricardo for helping me with the final stages of this project, the Leach family, and my karate family; Jacki L., the Moss's, the Yamasaki's, the Perrin's, the Brown's, and Roy C.

To Lindsay L., Juliet and Dan the Man. To Jason P. So-crates, Mikaela S. and her letters from Japan, Paul V., J. Bean, Lindsay K., Vanessa T., Hayden M., Kassandra W., Brooke and Carlo, Makky and Sheryl K., Grant, Jessica P., and Pia Z.

To Officers Q.J., E.C., D.S., and S.B.

To Tim Powers and Derrick C. Brown whom I always promised I would mention in my first book. I am the writer I am today due to their inspiration.

Last but not least to Jennie. Thank you for tolerating my nonsense for so long and reminding me it's okay to be human.

Preface

      In August of 2010 I made very poor and stupid decisions that lead to the death of a beautiful and talented young woman. Individuals that were present and witnessed what occurred that tragic night tell a different version of events than those that have pieced together their own story. The details of that evening may be argued but the death of my dear friend is a cold hard fact. Hers was beauty that cannot be replicated nor replaced and on the night she died, a bright light of the world went out.

      As a result, I was ordered by the court to spend a year in a rehabilitation center followed by two years of incarceration in a detention facility. I failed her as a friend and whether or not redemption exists for me, it will now forever be my quest.

      On December 14, 2012 I turned myself in to the custody of the jail and wrote my first of many *haiku*. It was already evening when I arrived and it was early in the morning of December 3, 2014 when I was released. The intention of this book is to paint a larger picture of the two years spent in jail through small snapshots of everyday existence. I underwent many changes while detained and wanted to be able to trace my way back if I ever got lost on my journey.

Disclaimer

      I will be the first person to denounce these poems as anything resembling traditional *haiku*. One of the key characteristics of *haiku* is a *kigo* (季語) which is a seasonal reference. The following may adhere to the basic structural definition: three lines consisting of five syllables, seven syllables, and five syllables; but most are noticeably lacking the fundamental *kigo*. Please consider these simple three-lined poems merely for what they are as opposed to what they are not.

      To those readers that find my labeling these works as *haiku* unforgivable, I apologize sincerely but ask them to remember the wise words of one of Japan's greatest *haiku* writers, Matsuo Basho, "Do not follow in the footsteps of the old poets, seek what they sought."

      A quick note on pronunciation: As the pronunciation of a word reflects and determines the number of syllables it has, I found myself at a linguistic crossroads multiple times. Take for instance the word *fire* \'fir\, though the lexical entry may indicate one syllable, usage of the word can create more or less valid arguments whether this word is pronounced with a single or two syllables. Rather than split hairs and drive yourself crazy counting while you read, (as I may have done while I wrote), perhaps it would be best to simply relax and enjoy. Or not. It makes little difference…See there? *Difference* should reasonably be marked as having three syllables yet when spoken quickly I only hear two.

      Oh bother, here I go again.

Author's Note
On Walking the Four Roads:
      It is not possible to adhere to or follow every one of the rules set forth in these four different walks of life every moment of every day. As the Universe itself is "perfect", personal perfection is an illusion and a lie; whereas *Improvement* is reality and truth. To strive for perfection is to aim for an unobtainable goal but to seek improvement, even if only on small scales, is to take one step closer to Cosmic Alignment.
      One might ask, "If the Universe is perfect as it is, why should I seek to better myself?" The answer is that Universal Perfection is not a constant that can be measured. Therefore, the Truth as I understand it, can only be attained by reaching and then surpassing our own limitations.

"The Temple of Time; where Time is your God, your ultimate evil, your salvation and a worse cage than the metal bars that hold you there." ~*Tales from the Odd Odyssey of Zero*

12/14/2012
#1
Try to calm the soul
Tonight the Journey begins
First step has been made

12/15/2015
#2
Day one has begun
Everything around me, cold
People, Places, Things

#3
Can't tell when it's night
It just is or it is not
Can't rain all the Time

12/16/2012
#4
The coming winter
The warm embrace of loved ones
I'll just hug myself

#5
Morning and night Time
Difference cannot be seen
Nor can it be felt

12/17/2012
#6
Shouts of a drunk girl
Echoing down the hallway
This is no dorm room[49]

#7
Light in the darkness
Just take one step, then the next
Walking my Four Roads[1]

12/18/2012
#8
The clouds of winter
Smells of salt from the ocean
A man in a cage

#9
Because I have loved
I can say that I have lived
Will I live again?

12/19/2012
#10
Stiffness in my bones
Today feels like a long one
One step at a Time

#11
Surprising visits
A letter from T. Powers
Today: not too bad

12/20/2012
#12
Nothing else to do
I never much liked coffee
Only when I write

#13
Brief morning minutes
I saw no sunlight today
Time inches along

12/21/2012
#14
Crisp winter morning
Fine day for the world to end
I'm not that lucky [2]

12/22/12
#16
Could not sleep last night
Mind and body were fighting
Bags under my eyes

12/23/12
#18
Mornings are the worst.
Searching deep to find the strength,
That takes strength to find

12/24/12
#20
It's a strange feeling
To be trapped inside by rain
Mood reflects weather

12/25/12
#22
To rid myself of
Vanity and angry thoughts
I train and train more

12/26/12
#24
A leaf on the wind
But there is no wind blowing
Blocked by walls of fate

12/27/12
#26
Scales of the dragon
Even hell can be pretty
Sunshine on the trees

#15
If there is no cheese,
Why does the mouse run the maze?
Unanswerable

#17
A monk in training
Waiting for two years to pass
Caught in a Time warp

#19
Watching clouds float by
They have more substance than I
Can't ascend nor fly

#21
Will I be reborn
Into a phoenix that soars
Or remain ashes

#23
No one came today
Maybe they will tomorrow
Hope can be poison

#25
The cage of my mind
A darkness growing inside
No rain, no rainbows

#27
From this sad angle
I am not even able
To see the sunset

12/28/12
#28
Moment of weakness
Not ready to give up yet
Still have much to do

12/29/12
#30
I have always loved
Peanut butter and honey
Breakfast was tasty

12/30/12
#32
Dew covers the ground
The air is fresh, cool, and crisp.
Where is Paradise?

12/31/12
#34
Pink and purple clouds
A cool breeze of salty air
Jail in December

1/1/13
#36
The clouds are confused
The first crane flight of the year
There goes the second

1/2/13
#38
In dreams I am free
I did not want to wake up
Am I still asleep?

1/3/13
#40
Half moon in the West
The sun rising from the East
Birds sing good morning

#29
The Phoenix will rise
Dragon, Turtle, and Tiger
Will come in due Time

#31
The song of a hawk
Filled the winter sky today
Where are you off to?

#33
Blue, grey, and white skies
A light rain with a warm sun
California coast

#35
Blue sky, bright warm sun
Perfect day to end the year.
Why wait till midnight?

#37
I can see my breath
Why is Orion hiding?
No stars out tonight

#39
No visitors came
I had to clean up dog shit
What is for dinner?

#41
Drains were clogged today
The smell of shitty water
Doesn't bug the birds

1/4/13
#42
A frozen morning
The birds and the barbed wire
Both look very cold

1/5/13
#44
Turn back the sunlight
Just let me sleep all day long
Not like I'd miss much

1/6/13
#46
Frozen warriors
Another missed *kangeiko*
I hope they have thawed [3]

1/7/13
#48
As men in cages
We must ask first to shower
I need some fresh air

1/8/13
#50
A golden sunrise
Be quiet and let me sleep
Noisy hair clippers

1/9/13
#52
It is very hard
Not to dwell on better Times
Trapped in a vortex

1/10/13
#54
Screams and loud pounding
The best and worst wake up call
Someone shut him up

#43
January skies
I wish we had fireflies
To light up the night

#45
A tasty apple
Just enjoying happiness
Whenever present

#47
Look! My own tattoo!
Staring at the clouds shaped as
Koi fish yin and yang [4]

#49
Dragon in the clouds
Winter leaves with Autumn shades
A season of change

#51
The gears of my mind
Constantly turning today
Keeps them from rusting

#53
There's a good reason why
The *ka* in *karateka*
Is in *kazoku* [5]

#55
Ignore the clear skies
Feels like a storm is coming
A change in the wind

1/11/13
#56
Ignorance is bliss
Being relied on can suck
Trying not to stress

1/12/13
#58
Dark and scary dreams
A night of bad images
I just miss my friends

1/13/13
#60
I dream of far coasts
Trumpets sound from the distance
Spirit is breaking

1/14/13
#62
For men in a cage
Raised tempers are dangerous
Time for peace-keeping

1/15/13
#64
It's the little things
That can seem to cheer me up
Letter from Japan [6]

1/16/13
#66
Nothing to say yet
Positive thoughts, hard to find
Won't live forever

1/17/13
#68
Let compassion be
My second strongest weapon
And patience my first

#57
Shaving your own head
With low quality razors
Is a painful plan

#59
Flocks and flocks of geese
Kept honking as they flew by
The sunset's pink sky

#61
Courtyard at night Time
Staring out the same sky box
Hello, Jupiter

#63
Playing the fake role
Of a positive inmate.
Still dying inside

#65
A refreshing breeze
Away Westward to the beach
Oh, to be a leaf

#67
My eyes are too wide
And my mind is too narrow
For an optimist

#69
A much warmer day
Scents of SpringTime in the air
Dry but refreshing

1/18/13
#70
Brave little birdy
Came down to say good morning
Good? Well, we shall see.

1/19/13
#72
At twenty seven
My beard already shows signs
Of gray hair growing

1/20/13
#74
The goal of this life:
To create something lasting
So others can learn

1/21/13
#76
SomeTimes I only
Get to see the morning sky
Through a locked window

1/22/13
#78
Will it come to bloom?
A heart forever wilting
In Springless Winter

1/23/13
#80
Promises to keep
Honor I need to regain
Goals to accomplish

1/24/13
#82
Good and bad alike
Nothing will last forever
Just breathe and relax

#71
A winter season
Again coming to an end
What will SpringTime bring

#73
When my story ends
The proof of my existence
Will come from others

#75
It is not my job
To understand my pathway
Simply to walk it

#77
The stars are speaking
To me with forgotten words
I don't understand

#79
Ceiling of grey clouds
Finches gathering dinner
Winter still remains

#81
I used to wander
For my heart knew of no home
Home is the dojo

#83
Rain in the morning
Sunlight in the afternoon
Life on the West coast

1/25/13
#84
My legs keep moving
Walking down the same hallway
Each morning and night

1/26/13
#86
Singing loud all night
An orchestra of snoring
What awful music

1/27/13
#88
Dreams of adventure
Then waking up to a cell
And the day starts now

1/28/13
#90
A morning surprise
Greeted by two hummingbirds
Sharing the sunrise

1/29/13
#92
Which is the dream world?
Refusing reality,
Or waiting to die?

1/30/13
#94
Estranged body parts
Lack of communication
Between mind and heart

1/31/13
#96
When waking up to
Another day of this crap
Makes you crave your death

#85
A trusting nature
And a mistrusting instinct
A bipolar heart

#87
Too many pushups
An incredibly sore neck
Make for a bad day

#89
Letting Time pass by
Card games with old man Dennis
Just another day

#91
Derrick Brown spoke of
Black construction paper night
That is tonight's sky

#93
The weakness of man
Never ceases to amaze
Yet still confuses

#95
A channel showing
Japanese television
Brought me a smile

#97
A job to finish
My soul seeks oblivion
Still have roads to walk

2/1/13
#98
Fifty days today
Emotional ebb and flow
Watching the sunrise

2/2/13
#100
Saturday morning
Reflecting on the past years
I've been trained for this

2/3/13
#102
Half-moon dead center
Dragon in the clouds again
Anticipation

2/4/13
#104
The smell of wet grass
A spectrum of emotions
Memories long gone

2/5/13
#106
Don't let dreams be dreams
Nothing is impossible
Not even wishes [8]

2/6/13
#108
Spirit of *kaizen*
Perfection does not exist
Strive for improvement [9]

2/7/13
#110
The fog rolls away
A grey morning on the coast
Rare patches of green

#99
Dancing hummingbirds
They wanted me to join them
Airborne emeralds

#101
The sky painted grey
A courtyard of grey metal
Where are the colors

#103
Losing track of Time
Reality spiraling
Up or down unknown

#105
The end of the world
Or the end of human kind
Just a waiting game

#107
Which is the real zoo,
Is it us inside this jail
Or the unseen cage?

#109
The faces of friends
Brief rays of light in the dark
Shadows come and go

#111
Running out of words
Repetition setting in
I fear stagnation

2/8/13
#112
Not sure if awake
Blinking eyes rapidly
Veil of consciousness

2/9/13
#114
Rejuvenated
A new book, a new journey
The page keeps turning

2/10/13
#116
Beautiful sunrise
Barely seen through breaking clouds
Morning paradox

2/11/13
#118
Birdsong wake up call
They do not wake us from sleep
Awake to a new life

2/12/13
#120
This is my great leap
Can or can't is not questioned
Questions come later

2/13/13
#122
Still in the dream world
The fog of reality
Stuck in my eyelids

2/14/13
#124
Sunrise solitude
It's lonely in the mountains
Lonely on the coast

#113
A sudden surprise
A letter from a past love
My heart has moved on

#115
Iceberg in the clouds
Pavilion where demons meet
Resting place for all

#117
Death comes to us all
The best and worst result
Nature's final debt

#119
Be complete in life
Be complete in all you do
Be complete in death

#121
Hold your two hands up
Stare through the window they make
The bigger picture

#123
We are all robots
Living based on programming
My circuits are fried

#125
Building new fences
I hope the birds don't fly off
I would miss their songs

2/15/13
#126
Cellmates come and go
No tears shed for faceless names
We are just numbers

2/16/13
#128
The past depresses
Thought of the future frustrates
Living in the now

2/17/13
#130
One two three four five
Seven syllables go here
Five four three two one

2/18/13
#132
Timeless as the Earth
Will friends pass the test of Time
I hope they will wait

2/19/13
#134
Voices and shadows
Wandering through the darkness
No one holds my hand

2/20/13
#136
Origami cranes
Focusing on the paper
One fold at a Time

2/21/13
#138
Today makes ten weeks
Such a beautiful morning
A day for writing

#127
The question remains
Is the fence to keep me in
Or to keep you out

#129
Rainbow colored sky
Last few minutes of sunset
Western lullaby

#131
Robots shed no tears
Stuffed animals cannot cry
The sea does not weep

#133
Weird sort of day dreams
Odd memories returning
My thought train derailed

#135
Daily reflection
Four Roads and thirty-nine rules
Breathe in and breathe out

#137
All things rise and fall
Past, Future, and Forever
There is only Now

#139
Ship tossed on the sea
Sailing for the horizon
No wave will stop me

2/22/13
#140
A state of limbo
Revelation in my dreams
Riding out the storm

2/23/13
#142
Damn monotony
Dreams are my only escape
A grumpy morning

2/24/13
#144
Forcing syllables
Forgetting to let them flow
Writing is no chore

2/25/13
#146
Shadowed silhouette
The sun rising and setting
Marks one day closer

2/26/13
#148
A warriors test
Peace in the midst of chaos
Attacked from all sides

2/27/13
#150
The drum in my chest
Percussion against my ribs
The music of life

2/28/13
#152
This is not living
This is merely surviving
Hurry up and wait

#141
A wondering mind
Where would I be, if not here?
A wandering mind

#143
A midnight voyage
Being guided by moonbeams
Gone from solid ground

#145
The game is afoot
This is no coincidence
Right place and right Time

#147
Big Brother's watching
Cameras on the ceiling
Never blinking eyes

#149
Is sin contagious?
Will evil latch on to me?
Can I wash it off?

#151
My muse is absent
Writing feels forced and pointless
Lack of rhapsody

#153
My mind will be strong
My resolve will be solid
My heart will be brave

3/1/13
#154
Can't focus my mind
Lack of sleep, taking its toll
Failing to form thought

#155
Coming and going
Like a hamster on the wheel
Round and round again

3/2/13
#156
Abrasive cellmate
Walking a different path
Yet we both met here

#157
Lost in the four suits
Cups, swords, wands, and pentacles
The cards are shuffled

3/3/13
#158
Frozen and alone
Self-fulfilling prophecy
Written in the ice

#159
In a frozen cave
Chained by thoughts and memories
There the demon sleeps

3/4/13
#160
Dreamt about the past
She was my Tiny Dancer
But she danced away

#161
Warrior poet
Though my honor will remain
My heart may wither

3/5/13
#162
It's a lonely quest
Perhaps today's lesson is
To pick myself up

#163
A bond through hardship
Friends in unlikely places
Seal Beach redemption

3/6/13
#164
Complaints from small minds
Like mosquitoes in summer
Constantly buzzing

#165
Stress will be deadly
Relax. You will live longer
Remember to breathe

3/7/13
#166
Frustrating cellmate
I should practice what I preach
He's not worth my Time

#167
The mountain is high
My legs are sore from climbing
I want to give up

3/8/13
#168
Disturbing nightmares
Disturbing reality
Not much difference

3/9/13
#170
A chorus of frogs
Singing and croaking all night
A green serenade

3/10/13
#172
Daylight Savings Time
Fall back, Spring forward, lose sleep
Tell that to the sun

3/11/13
#174
Here we go again
Another Monday morning
Are you still reading?

3/12/13
#176
Foggy breath and mist
Like walking through a daydream
Footprints on asphalt

3/13/13
#178
In an hour glass
I am just one grain of sand
Prey to gravity

3/14/13
#180
Some mornings are slow
Others seem to go by fast
It's all in my head

#169
A passing rain cloud
A downpour for thirsty plants
First flowers of Spring

#171
Juliet and Dan
Epitome of sunshine
Brought my smile back

#173
Trapped in a cycle
Wake up, eat, stare at the wall
Sleep, and then repeat

#175
Just another day
Nothing new to write about
No motivation

#177
The bloom of Spring Time
Color in a sea of grey
Darkness comes and goes

#179
Pray and prey alike
A pawn of the Universe
Transcendental fate

#181
A fear of the dark
A dim light in a dark place
Can go a long way

3/15/13
#182
All my adventures
Have brought me to here and now
Unpredictable

#183
The human spirit
Outlasts and overpowers
The human body

3/16/13
#184
Tensions will be high
Too many men in one cell
Hope nothing happens

#185
I am exhausted
Patience uses energy
Today has drained me

3/17/13
#186
Student of the world
Cursed or blessed to walk alone
What's today's lesson

#187
Don't tell Ireland
Orange on Saint Patrick's Day
Almost blasphemy

3/18/13
#188
Learning to let go
Grasping onto last night's dream
Sand through my fingers

#189
No sense of normal
Constant changes to routine
Must learn to adapt

3/19/13
#190
Struggling to write
Unable to form new words
Have I said this yet?

#191
Using my fingers
Always counting syllables
I must look silly

3/20/13
#192
Elusive nightmares
Scary enough to lose sleep,
But not remember

#193
Life in a bubble
Does the real world still exist
If it ever did

3/21/13
#194
Juggling tensions
Seeking homeostasis
Can't find a balance

#195
Love and suffering
Go together hand in hand
My hand is empty

3/22/13
#196
It comes full circle
The lessons I never learned
Are what I need now

3/23/13
#198
Beauty still exists
For now only in my mind
My only reprieve

3/24/13
#200
I dreamt of Venice
A pretty girl named Diane
On the Scalzzi Bridge[11]

3/25/13
#202
Musical bird friend
Serenades me each morning
Sarah the robin[12]

3/26/13
#204
A two way mirror
Reflecting a reflection
That is what I am

3/27/13
#206
I will miss my beard
I have grown attached to it
No pun intended

3/28/13
#208
Yet another day
Ran out of books yesterday
Boredom will ensue[13]

#197
Metamorphosis
The ultimate warrior
My transformation

#199
Such a lucky find
A flower among the weeds
A hidden beauty

#201
A moment of pause
In the airport of my life
Just a layover

#203
Where days feel like weeks
Weeks feel as long as a day
No real sense of Time

#205
Advice from the past
As my grandma used to say
Keep on keeping on

#207
Must not lose my Way
Vacation from vocation
Unacceptable

#209
Not knowing the words
To a song stuck in your head
Can drive you crazy

3/29/13
#210
This is my battle
All have a dragon to slay
Can't let it beat you

3/30/13
#212
When the Time is right
A warrior needs to rest
Sensible tactics

3/31/13
#214
Trapped in a low tide
Walking on the shore of Fate
Can't swim out to sea

4/1/13
#216
Wrestling with dreams
Running away to Japan
Leave this life behind

4/2/13
#218
Labeled a villain
The ironies of my life
Chance to rise above

4/3/13
#220
A spirit of wind
Trapped in this flesh and bone cage
Dreaming of the sky

4/4/13
#222
A long sea voyage
Looking for the horizon
Sailing through the storm

#211
A constant dulling
My sword as well as my wit
Developing rust

#213
The demons get loud
When no one comes to visit
Perhaps it's nap Time

#215
Basking in the sun
Hot asphalt under my back
The last day of March

#217
Window in the clouds
Seeing through to the blue side
A glimpse of heaven

#219
My daily routine
Reading, writing, exercise
My monastery

#221
I made a new friend
A grasshopper in the weeds
He went on his way

#223
An anchored body
Wishing to dance in moonlight
My soul wanders on

4/5/13
#224
Watching inmates leave
One day I will feel that joy
But for now I wait

4/6/13
#226
On that fateful night
I failed to protect my friend
Now she protects me

4/7/13
#228
Tossing and turning
A night full of restless sleep
Waking up groggy

4/8/13
#230
I can't go outside
Because "it's too windy"
Nothing but nonsense

4/9/13
#232
Lights on at seven
Breakfast at seven thirty
Bored by eight o'clock

4/10/13
#234
Enclosed by four walls
My perception of the world
Shrinking day by day

4/11/13
#236
Outline of houses
The other side of the fence
May as well be fake

#225
When chasing a dream
Turns into chasing nightmares
It's Time to wake up

#227
Time to move forward
Attachment to my old self
Will just hold me back

#229
Flame of existence
Like a smoldering ember
Or an inferno

#231
Striving for greatness
Dedication to a goal
Day in and day out

#233
No need to worry
The Universe will provide
No more and no less

#235
Jacki and Henry
My second mom and brother
Black belt family

#237
Don't ask yourself why
Instead, ask yourself why not
It changes the world

4/12/13
#238
The passing of Time
Everything in nature
It all fades to grey

4/13/13
#240
My dreams are wild
If I could charge admission
I would be quite rich

4/14/13
#242
That which I despise
Is the one thing I am best at
Daily survival

4/15/13
#244
No hero's welcome
My return will be humble
Monks need no glory

4/16/13
#246
Searching for answers
The hidden meaning in dreams
A wild goose chase

4/17/13
#248
My body needs rest
My mind just wants to wake up
Trapped in sleep limbo

4/18/13
#250
As Jacki would say
A cookie in the oven
But on the right track

#239
Facing my demons
Spilling my guts on the page
Answering the call

#241
An act of kindness
Can make all the difference
Bad days become good

#243
One does not know faith
Until that faith is tested
What do I believe

#245
The question remains
Am I seeking righteousness
Or running from fear

#247
Whispers in the wind
Swaying branches speak to me
The leaves have secrets

#249
Shields can be broken
Love strengthens what honor can't
But leaves deeper scars

#251
Mind over matter
Advice from my friend Henry
Lesson to live by

4/19/13
#252
Change happens so fast
Don't take loved ones for granted
Enjoy little things

#253
Just go with the flow
Like water off a duck's back
Let it roll off you

4/20/13
#254
For now, this is home
Spirit of the wanderer
My wings have been clipped

#255
Cross the finish line
The last steps are the hardest
A true marathon

4/21/13
#256
No inspiration
The birds continue to sing
A day like the rest

#257
Life is just a game
We were not made to suffer
We have chosen to

4/22/13
#258
Enjoy this hardship
Universal perfection
All things have a place

#259
Before I knew it
The day has already passed
Another one gone

4/23/13
#260
Mist lands on my neck
A crane flying overhead
The day has started

#261
SomeTimes I miss it
A lie to say otherwise
Life of decadence

4/24/13
#262
Shocking images
A dream with cryptic meaning
Hell is in your mind

#263
Where is the sunshine
It seemed that summer was here
The weather has changed

4/25/13
#264
Sunrise and sunset
The world continues to turn
What will today bring

#265
Surfing the cosmos
Facing the darkness head on
Emptiness of space

4/26/13
#266
Light in the darkness
A source of warmth for the cold
Someone to walk with

4/27/13
#268
Calendar days pass
Another inmate departs
Rejoin the real world

4/28/13
#270
Unable to sleep
The dream world eluded me
No escape last night

4/29/13
#272
Without any sleep
The motivation to write
Is harder to find

4/30/13
#274
The goal of training
Turn weaknesses into strengths
I am on that path

5/1/13
#276
Child of the Earth
My pillow is made of stone
A bed of soft dirt

5/2/13
#278
New book idea
My hand can't write fast enough
Need ink and coffee

#267
A soothing Spring wind
The newly bloomed flowers dance
Swaying back and forth

#269
My heart seeks the truth
The sacred art of writing
Lost in endless words

#271
Change of scenery
New faces arriving
Welcome to the show

#273
A small victory
Finally beat the crossword
Exercised my brain

#275
Dance with destiny
Laugh in the face of your doubts
Create your own fate

#277
Five visits today
Friends came from around the world
Can't stop smiling

#279
Training together
A lizard doing pushups
As I was jogging

5/3/13
#280
A flower and weeds
Struggling for the same dirt
Growing side by side

#281
The moon speaks to me
The loneliness of the sky
The stars feel it too

5/4/13
#282
Someone cries at night
First Time being arrested
Tears in the darkness

#283
Human emotions
A confusing paradox
Breakable yet strong

5/5/13
#284
Never would have guessed
Jared and Megan showed up
A happy surprise

#285
Life is a treadmill
It runs with or without you
Don't lose your footing

5/6/13
#286
I am no artist
I have no grand delusions
My poems need work

#287
Five minutes of sun
A sudden summer downpour
Watering the plants

5/7/13
#288
Yesterday is gone
Tomorrow is tomorrow
Today is Today

#289
Rain in the morning
Sunshine in the afternoon
Stars come out at night

5/8/13
#290
Keep my mind guessing
A comfortable routine
Creates illusions

#291
Windows to the soul
Staring into the mirror
I don't see a thing

5/9/13
#292
Patience and action
Both have a specific Time
Know the difference

#293
I need to slow down
Don't forget that haste makes waste
There's no need to rush

5/10/13
#294
Enlightening talks
Too early in the morning
Send my head spinning

5/11/13
#296
Pebbles and mountains
In the end they are the same
Step over or climb

5/12/13
#298
Ruffle no feathers
The wind can be treacherous
Help others to fly

5/13/13
#300
Stressful vibrations
Too tired to really care
Electric tensions

5/14/13
#302
The fog of a dream
Continues to cloud my eyes
Even when awake

5/15/13
#304
Today has promise
Visitors from all over
Staying positive

5/16/13
#306
Falling into line
Ants will work diligently
All life has a place

#295
Each blessing a curse
And each curse is a blessing
Just be creative

#297
I need to focus
Reevaluate my goals
Where do I go now

#299
Another tally
One hundred and fifty days
Nineteen months to go

#301
A constant current
As unsteady as the sea
Riding on the waves

#303
God flicks his finger
Universal dominos
Falling into place

#305
Sun-bathing lizard
Cool breeze to keep the heat off
Not a cloud in sight

#307
A nagging questions
Everyday I am stronger
What is my purpose

5/17/13
#308
Dreaming of rescue
From the prison of my mind
Who has the spare key?

5/18/13
#310
Silence is golden
Cacophony of snoring
No peace during sleep

5/19/13
#312
I stared at my bunk
And waited all night for dreams
But none came to me

5/20/13
#314
Into the Unknown
Face your battles with courage
Keep your head up high

5/21/13
#316
Riding on moonbeams
Trying to outrun the night
Here comes the sunrise

5/22/13
#318
Picking up the pen
Just going through the motions
Ink and paper meet

5/23/13
#320
Ants don't ask questions
They just understand their place
I do not know mine

#309
Old wounds are healing
Scars returning to fresh skin
Pain helps us to learn

#311
The eye of the storm
Do not be fooled by the calm
Be ready for waves

#313
No mas Alonso
Adios mi amigo
Ay que lastima

#315
Destroy who you are
Use the pieces to rebuild
Stronger than before

#317
Darkest before dawn
The sunrise still eludes me
Waiting for daybreak

#319
I can be grumpy
Jennie gave me permission
For one day only [14]

#321
Destroying nature
The atrocities of Man
False security

5/24/13
#322
I speak no deceit
I someTimes withhold the truth
Lies of omission

5/25/13
#324
My monotony
Melatonin induced dreams
Absurd premises

5/26/13
#326
I roll out of bed
Will this be the day I die
Make the best of it

5/27/13
#328
Avoid the mundane
Each day has a special gift
Always search for it

5/28/13
#330
On the cosmic road
My chariot awaits me
Into the night sky

5/29/13
#332
A slow start morning
Can't wipe the sleep from my eyes
Just go back to sleep

5/30/13
#334
All of this support
I must have done something right
I won't let them down

#323
The devil you know
Is better to deal with than
The devil you don't

325
Be right or happy
You only get to choose one
You cannot be both

#327
A love of shadows
Addicted to tragedy
A poet's weakness

#329
Embrace inner strength
Change is inevitable
Grab on, don't let go

#331
Repeated mistakes
Some people will never learn
What about myself

#333
So many faces
Ever changing as the wind
Which is the real me

#335
The world quickly turns
One can only go forward
Before going back

5/31/13
#336
So cold in this cell
They claim it is to kill germs
Can't seem to get warm

6/1/13
#338
Moving like a snail
Watching the minutes tick by
Some mornings are slow

6/2/13
#340
Veil of emotion
The moment of clarity
That comes with hindsight

6/3/13
#342
Time to face the day
I blink as the lights come on
Which is the dream world?

6/4/13
#344
I walk with demons
So I can fly with angels
The truth, or a lie

6/5/13
#346
The race yet to come
Starting over from zero
Excitement and dread

6/6/13
#348
Repeating the speech
Welcoming the newcomers
Shut up and be clean

#337
Anachronism
From the past and the future
Yet I am here now

#339
Making new contacts
Bringing people together
Expanding networks

#341
Running in circles
Like a dog without a home
Chasing my own tail

#343
As inmate P. says
It is just another day
Another dollar

#345
Too many questions
With no answers to be found
No point in asking

#347
Still soaring higher
On the winds of destiny
No place to land yet

#349
I did not like that
Being stared at by students
Like an animal[15]

6/7/13
#350
Penance for my sins
Sitting locked inside my head
No more soft living

6/8/13
#352
I can't look away
Little finch in the dead grass
Eating seeds for lunch

6/9/13
#354
Though I may stumble
There is no turning back now
I walk the Four Roads [1]

6/10/13
#356
Doors slamming all night
People making too much noise
No sleep to be found

6/11/13
#358
Making slow progress
Two steps forward, one step back
The Jail Time Shuffle

6/12/13
#360
Your voice hinders you
Be quiet and learn to see
Answers are all there

6/13/13
#362
My priorities
What exactly are they now,
And what will they be?

#351
These are my haiku
Grammatical traditions
Get no say in it

#353
Watching a spider
Wrap its web around a meal
Are June-bugs tasty?

#355
What did today cost?
Every day has a debt
Have I paid in full?

#357
A mental escape
Living in a fantasy
Anywhere but here

#359
Six months completed
A quarter of the way through
Eighteen months to go

#361
Mist against my cheek
The loneliness of June Gloom
Clouds for company

#363
Edge of a plateau
Does it only level out
Or keep going up

26

6/14/13
#364
It could not be helped
I missed the cherry blossoms
Winter in Japan

6/15/13
#366
Island of my mind
No ship on the horizon
Far too far to swim

6/16/13
#368
I stare at the sky
Listen to the world spinning
All people as one

6/17/13
#370
I love watching ants
A straight forward existence
Ignorance is bliss

6/18/13
#372
Always transforming
The eclectic eccentric
Never the same twice

6/19/13
#374
Waking up to peace
Once again an empty cell
Enjoy it for now

6/20/13
#376
A minute ticks by
The days are going slower
How long till sunset?

#365
Tears hide in the rain
I used to love rainy days
No more tears, just rain

#367
On visiting day
The warmth a smile can bring
Would conquer all frost

#369
I do not deny
That I wish I died that night
But I must live on

#371
Thought precedes action
Action determines outcome
Honor needs no thought

#373
I may not like it
But I don't need to like it
I am here to learn

#375
A void in my heart
A folly to fill the hole
The pain helps me feel

#377
As each day passes
One day closer to the end
Which end will that be?

6/21/13
#378
A tale to be told
Two small ants so far off course
On an adventure

6/22/13
#380
What the hell is that?
A mysterious white dot
Floating in the sky

6/23/13
#382
The highest practice
Is to serve other gladly
I am not there yet

6/24/13
#384
It was too easy
Muscles need to burn to grow
They are burning now

6/25/13
#386
Running in circles
Looking back to move forward
Going nowhere fast

6/26/13
#388
Different footprints
All paths cross for a reason
Take a walk with me

6/27/13
#390
Manna from heaven
First cup of tea in six months
A glorious thing

#379
Fear no drastic change
It is the way of the world
Hold on and enjoy

#381
Ripples on a lake
From peaceful to chaotic
Temple under siege

#383
The pain of sad songs
SomeTimes teaches a lesson
Remember to live

#385
This story of mine
Is just like all epic tales
It needs an ending

#387
They are not the same
Patience and hesitation
Never hesitate

#389
A long road to walk
I have promises to keep
I want to move on

#391
A few feet of space
Changes a room to a cell
That, and metal bars

6/28/13
#392
For hundreds of years
Martial arts hid in dance moves
I hide them in chores [16]

6/29/13
#394
Surface perceptions
Be still as a frozen lake
Flowing underneath

6/30/13
#396
Pursuits of the mind
I excelled when I was young
Now playing catch up

7/1/13
#398
Lonely concrete walls
Thirty seven steps to light
Outside but fenced in

7/2/13
#400
In the middle ground
Expect the best and the worst
Never a surprise

7/3/13
#402
I hate to admit
That I was defeated by
A jigsaw puzzle

7/4/13
#404
Brotherhood of one
Other will join me in Time
For now I will wait

#393
Stay out of trouble
Grab a mop and look busy
The Jerry technique [17]

#395
Why does the wolf cry
A lonely song in the night
The moon went away

#397
Self contemplation
An exhausting enterprise
Will these seeds bear fruit?

#399
Me, myself, and I
Loneliness can be freeing
No need to pretend

#401
Some call me stubborn
Unwillingness to settle
Is what I call it

#403
In my darker days
I spoke of 'Bar-room Angels'
Angels in disguise

#405
Greet all that you meet
As a fellow traveler
All souls have a path

7/5/13
#406
Seek the world beyond
I will not fear what comes next
Once my tasks are done

7/6/13
#408
Visions of the past
Memories long forgotten
New stories await

7/7/13
#410
Freedom or escape
Chained down by past memories
My own worst prison

7/8/13
#412
Muses old and new
Please guide this pen to be true
Till my task is through

7/9/13
#414
Child of the light
That finds comfort in darkness
Between dusk and dawn

7/10/13
#416
There is no distance,
To find what I am seeking,
I would not travel

7/11/13
#418
Focusing on now
Thinking of the finish line
Still a long Time left

#407
You can't count pushups
And be sad at the same Time
A lucky loophole

#409
An inner battle
Claws gripping into my soul
Demons gaining ground

#411
This is not the end
As long as I don't give up
I will keep learning

#413
The sun was hiding
The clouds have been chased aw
Blue skies once again

#415
Bad habits return
Awful cliché poetry
Like back in high school

#417
My quest in the end
Will just lead me to myself
An inner journey

#419
A blissful moment
Listening to summer rain
Eating an apple

7/12/13
#420
Can't summon new words
When forced, the mind will constrict
Defeats the purpose

7/13/13
#422
No longer my choice
The path of least resistance
Is not an option

7/14/13
#424
On days like today
I can only see the fence
And nothing passed it

7/15/13
#426
"Me" of yesteryear
Uncompromising honor
What about "me" now?

7/16/13
#428
Mistakes have purpose
As long as you can learn from them
Long lost memories

7/17/13
#430
Face from the past
Haunting my dreams as I sleep
Unrequited love

7/18/13
#432
Regret not the past
What has happened cannot change
You are not in charge

#421
Don't dwell on what's lost
Press forward with no regrets
Walk straight as a blade

#423
The price to be paid
All lessons come at a cost
Time is currency

#425
Ignorant of truth
What was the Forbidden Fruit
That brought consciousness

#427
With Venice sinking
I'm glad I got to see it
If only just once

#429
Battlefield of life
Adversity reveals truth
Do not fight the tide

#431
The paths not chosen
Could have led me anywhere
Destiny decides

#433
Learn to move forward
Do not live for tomorrow
Just live for today

7/19/13
#434
It was not a place
The true Garden of Eden
Was a state of mind

#435
Obsessed with numbers
Re-running calculations
Nothing adding up

7/20/13
#436
The cost of progress
Blacksmiths do not say sorry
To steel they hammer

#437
Sensei always says
Fall down eight Times, stand up nine
Time to stand again

7/21/13
#438
Playing dominos
A refreshing change of pace
Laughter soothes the soul

#439
The light of the moon
Glowing from behind the clouds
Picture perfect night

7/22/13
#440
Strength stems from the truth
To deny my weaknesses
Is to lose to them

#441
To defeat and pass
My human limitations
I must first find them

7/23/13
#442
Exercise your eyes
Close your mouth, open your mind
See before you speak

#443
Heavenly bodies
Even in meditation
There is no stillness

7/24/13
#444
Cool air on my skin
The breeze blowing through the fence
Where does the wind rest?

#445
Feeling pretty low
The prison fence in my mind
Grew an inch taller

7/25/13
#446
A funny feeling
Even in the summer heat
Loneliness is cold

#447
On kitchen duty
Watching bread turn into toast
An exciting life

7/26/13
#448
Vibrant red and green
A ladybug on a leaf
Nature's sharp contrast

7/27/13
#450
No more center stage
Fading into the background
Final curtain call

7/28/13
#452
This cell may be small
But a closed mind is smaller
I prefer this cage

7/29/13
#454
Walk through the desert
If you make it to heaven
Your feet will still burn

7/30/13
#456
With turbulent thoughts
I no longer know myself
What will I become?

7/31/13
#458
No recognition
Stranger in the reflection
With the same green eyes

8/1/13
#460
Facing decisions
Excuses are empty words
Action carries proof

#449
Getting lost in thought
Harder to find my way back
Redrawing the map

#451
Food from outside
Chicken, coleslaw, and pulled pork
A happy stomach [18]

#453
Though this is a test
The waiting is easier
Than what is to come

#455
Smile with each task
Universal karmic law
Governs all of us

#457
Tension in the room
Mask of positivity
All so tiring

#459
Much needed surprise
A visit from Lindsay K.
Lifted my spirits

#461
Fishy aroma
The breeze is the breath of god
He needs a breath mint

8/2/13
#462
Yesterday's Maiku
Is my only opponent
Him and only him

8/3/13
#464
Glories of the past
Hold no weight in the present
Starting from zero

8/4/13
#466
All bound together
Sorrow is Universal
Known to all mankind

8/5/13
#468
When down in a ditch
It takes outside perspective
To climb out again

8/6/13
#470
Man's complexities
I thought I could read people
Still illiterate

8/7/13
#472
For Mai and mom's sake
I miss the smell of roses
A scent of beauty

8/8/13
#474
Scars tell my story
Four screw-holes around my skull
Hard not to notice [21]

#463
Ignoring inmates
Another form of training
My dojo mojo [19]

#465
Admit your mistakes
Needed an eye opener
Hope it's not too late

#467
Pain is guaranteed
Suffering is optional
Depends on your mind

#469
It's impossible
You can't hate a Beatles fan
"All you need is love" [20]

#471
Try to instill hope
Break linguistic barriers
Smiles always help

#473
Smooth skin is useless
Love me for my calluses
Or don't waste your Time

#475
With matching tempers
My biggest obstacle yet
Not losing control

34

8/9/13
#476
Repressing dark thoughts
Does not make them disappear
They strive in darkness

8/10/13
#478
The deep waters call
Traveling through black tunnels
Darkness overwhelms

8/11/13
#480
Concerning people:
Do not care more than you must
But love them fully

8/12/13
#482
On the Today Show
Seal Beach Jail celebrity
Never trust the news

8/13/13
#484
Like a parasite
I feel the claws of demons
Latching on to me

8/14/13
#486
Releasing toxins
Beads of sweat on my forehead
Muscles shedding tears

8/15/13
#488
Knowing when to rest
Is a part of training too
For now, I push on

#477
A false sense of pride
The shame of being human
Apathetic lies

#479
Bonds made through friendship
Some are stronger than others
Always be thankful

#481
Negative feelings
Wrapping their chains around me
Trying to break free

#483
Dancing through the leaves
Coasting on the coastal winds
Wishes made at night

#485
I can't remember
What it feels like to smile
And really mean it

#487
Shimmer of white light
Hope still exists within me
A poison's own cure

#489
Wanted my haiku
To avoid repetition
But jail is just that

8/16/13
#490
My mind drifts away
Not gone but not here either
Mingling with the clouds

8/17/13
#492
A hard fact of life
Tragedy as an art form
Seduces us all

8/18/13
#494
I missed the off ramp
The road to enlightenment
Is the other way

8/19/13
#496
Just biding my Time
And waiting for my return
To where, and as what?

8/20/13
#498
Met a two year goal
One hundred thousand pushups
In less than nine months

8/21/13
#500
Inner tornado
Can't seem to focus my thoughts
Make it through the day

8/22/13   22
#502
She left forever
Three years ago on this day
The loss is still felt

#491
Water on asphalt
Evaporating puddles
Steam transformation

#493
Old priorities
Now is not the Time for wants
It is Time for needs

#495
When you pray to God
You can't always wait for help
You must help yourself

#497
Another circle
My foolish quest for meaning
Has led me to here

#499
Keep the ones you like
Not all haiku will be gems
The rest fade away

#501
I just want to go
Where no one can follow me
Into my own mind

#503
A day of silence
For those who can speak no mor
Gone, not forgotten

8/23/13
#504
Nothing set in stone
Justice is a perspective
No consistency

8/24/13
#506
Right next to the beach
But unable to get there
So close, yet so far

8/25/13
#508
The changing weather
Another season passes
Fall is on the way

8/26/13
#510
If asked honestly
I see no happy ending
The story just ends

8/27/13
#512
Sleep still fills my eyes
The real world and the dream world
Are one and the same

8/28/13
#514
I don't want to write
I don't want to exercise
I don't want to want

8/29/13
#516
Not a play on words
Meaningless without meaning
Just a place holder

#505
Waiting is the game
All I ever do is wait
Time just passes by

#507
Put reins on your fate
Grab the wind and ride away
Challenge destiny

#509
If you have the Time
To come up with an excuse
Shut up, get to work

#511
My reason to live
Something still obscure
Tired of asking

#513
One goal at this point
To leave with my head held high
Return still intact

#515
The motive was good
But motivational lies
Will just cause setbacks

#517
There is no winning
Just seeing how long it takes
For the game to end

8/30/13
#518
My cell may be cold
But the world is warm outside
Time to face the day

8/31/13
#520
Dense humidity
Surrounding and embracing
A hug from the air

9/1/13
#522
Lost among the leaves
Wishes and dreams float away
Food for demons

9/2/13
#524
No body or voice
To exist as an echo
Recite. Float away.

9/3/13
#526
Dirt won't always stain
One hand washes the other
Become clean again

9/4/13
#528
Dive into the page
No preparation needed
The words find themselves

9/5/13
#530
Time passes you by
The land of the forgotten
No trace will be left

#519
Lizards in the yard
They watch me as I watch them
Enjoying the sun

#521
Cycle of rebirth
Larva, cocoon, butterfly
Which stage am I in?

#523
Connecting star dots
Intersections and crossroads
Cosmic alignment

#525
A two sided coin
One cannot know purity
Without knowing sin

#527
Changing points of view
Distorted reality
There is no, 'One Truth'

#529
Goals are like gardens
Can't always keep the weeds out
Prepare to regrow

#531
What may hurt the limb
Can someTimes aid the body
For the greater good

9/6/13
#532
Days pass one by one
The walls start to stare at you
Dust becomes your friend

#533
New discovery
Presented forms of myself
A choice must be made

9/7/13
#534
Don't erase the past
A great tree comes from strong roots
All from just one seed

#535
Japanese beetle
Where are you off to today?
Find yourself some shade

9/8/13
#536
With a mop and broom
What was dirty becomes clean
Souls are much like floors

#537
Heart can collect dust
Brush them off, get them beating
The drum in your chest

9/9/13
#538
Plans drawn in the sand
The waves will wipe the slate clean
It's not high tide yet

#539
A near empty jail
An inmate wanders the halls
Rare moment of peace

9/10/13
#540
Consistent only
In lack of consistency
Nothing stays the same

#541
Shadow of myself
I was never a great man
But what am I now?

9/11/13
#542
Cracks in the cement
Dust collecting on metal
Wrinkles in the sheets

#543
Cracks in my spirit
Dust collecting on my heart
Wrinkles on my brow

9/12/13
#544
A long dark tunnel
Without lights to lead the way
Small tentative steps

#545
Orange uniforms
Nine months of wearing orange
Need a color change

9/13/13
#546
The doors slam at night
Over and over again
Hallways never rest

9/14/13
#548
Wall of fog outside
Ice crystals hang in the air
All Time seems to stop

9/15/13
#550
Spiders spinning webs
Morning dew clings to the strands
Gems in the courtyard

9/16/13
#552
Logical thinking
Receives no warm welcomes here
Just smile and nod

9/17/13
#554
In an empty shell
A disappearing spirit
A soul spread too thin

9/18/13
#556
Morning overcast
No wall of fog to speak of
The trees are asleep

9/19/13
#558
Metallic haiku
A small window of nature
Lacking a heartbeat

#547
Sterilize the walls
The smell of disinfectant
All over the cells

#549
Into the dead zone
Grains of sand through your fingers
Broken hourglass

#551
Off-white stucco walls
Dull and rust grey metal
A colorless day

#553
Grey and white decor
Cell one, bunk two is my home
Dust bunnies as pets

#555
Think objectively
The sun is shining somewhere
Even if not here

#557
The gift of a crane
An origami kindess
Flying on wishes

#559
Despite open eyes
One sees what they want to see
Regardless of truth

9/20/13
#560
A curse not a gift
Intelligent but not wise
Aimless wanderer

#561
Hi Mr. Cockroach
Sorry, but you must leave now
You are not welcome

9/21/13
#562
Unstable footing
Pyramid of emotion
One block at a Time

#563
Sudden blue to grey
The sky is playing with me
Mercurial bitch

9/22/13
#564
An ironic path
S.J.B. to S.B.J.
Trapped in my own fate[23]

#565
Helping to direct
The face behind the curtain
Fitting puzzle piece

9/23/13
#566
Due to apathy
The demon is gaining ground
That, or laziness

#567
Harder to escape
A cell made inside your mind
Than a cage of steel

9/24/13
#568
Walking through my dreams
Someone that used to smile
Walks along side me

#569
Beads of sweat roll off
Try to banish the demons
They always return

9/25/13
#570
Move on, tumble weed
No place for you to plant roots
Just keep on rolling

#571
All good things must end
One less thing for which I hope
Now where do I turn

9/26/13
#572
Another Thursday
Sixty-two weeks remaining
How fast will it go

#573
A balancing act
The line between light and dark
Pit falls on both sides

9/27/13
#574
All people will die
An inescapable fate
Not all truly live

9/28/13
#576
You may not agree
Success is love and respect
Not in dollar signs

9/29/13
#578
Endless masquerade
Deceiving even myself
Hiding my true face

9/30/13
#580
Emptiness is cold
It is not absence or void
A frozen vacuum

10/1/13
#582
Scary to stand still
Say goodbye to the bad things
Scary to move on

10/2/13
#584
Brief oblivion
To the gates of Hell and back
Comforting darkness

10/3/13
#586
Now repelled by both
Shadows used to comfort me
The light burns my eyes

#575
Lacking what I need
For myself, not from others
What is it they see?

#577
Outline of shoulders
Watching someone walk away
A tragic beauty

#579
Feathers fill the sky
Flying in a 'V' formation
The geese have returned

#581
Autumn is ending
The last day of September
Feels quite like July

#583
Where does the wind sleep?
Does it have a bed of clouds,
To welcome it home?

#585
In a world of ice
Nothing is warmer than love
Sorrows melt away

#587
I am far away
In the pages of a book
Beyond space and Time

10/4/13
#588
Laugh at irony
SomeTimes it's the only choice
Laugh and feel less pain

10/5/13
#590
Why bother breathing
If not improving in life
Standing still is death

10/6/13
#592
Words without reason
Apathetic poetry
Polluting the page

10/7/13
#594
Roaming with no goal
Lost in thought without a map
Don't care to return

10/8/13
#596
Lukewarm cup of tea
Something to start the day with
Dawn meditation

10/9/13
#598
I speak of the dawn
But cannot see through these walls
Blind hope for the sun

10/10/13
#600
Tiny lizard friend
Glad I did not step on you
Catch bugs and grow big

#589
At Times of weakness
Don't give the demons playTime
They won't take a nap

#591
Dryness in the air
Brown leaves collect on the ground
Death before rebirth

#593
Balloon on the wind
Carried away from small hands
Drifting to new heights

#595
The year presses on
Fighting an uphill battle
Need to take a breath

#597
Memory of naps
In the hidden bamboo trees
Cal State Fullerton [25]

#599
Eyes fixed to the ground
Cost of sleep deprivation
Can't finish this line

#601
All roads can't be seen
SomeTimes helping, makes things worse
Shrug and keep walking

10/11/13
#602
Which tree is better?
The strong oak falls to the wind
And the willow bends

10/12/13
#604
Old habits die hard
A new me in a new world
The old world is gone

10/13/13
#606
Polite guards aside
Here, we are just animals
Not seen as human

10/14/13
#608
If given a chance
Some people may surprise you
Don't hold your breath though

10/15/13
#610
This guy is something
Even Buddha would slap him
I tried to be nice

10/16/13
#612
Only felt alive
When I was killing myself
All are born to live

10/17/13
#614
Crisp air in my lungs
The mornings are cooling down
October sunrise

#603
The majority
And those with authority
Decide what is sane

#605
I'm sure he means well
Some people just love to talk
Does he ever quit?

#607
Blue skies and storm clouds
Such a beautiful contrast
Canvas of nature

#609
Dislike of others
Is a reflective viewpoint
Love more and judge less

#611
Go down and push up
Over and over again
Grow stronger each day

#613
A voice from the trees
An invisible songbird
Good day to you too

#615
Carefree gust of wind
A leaf floating in the sky
Must come down someTime

10/18/13
#616
Pink and gold sunrise
Strange place for beautiful sights
In a world of gray

#617
Carrot cake and cheese
Food based metaphors for life
Still unsavory [26]

10/19/13
#618
Denial of truth
Will not protect you from it
Rejection of life

#619
Counting passing cars
Nothing more disappointing
Waiting for no one

10/20/13
#620
Sick joke of nature
Go to sleep, wake up older
Youth ticking away

#621
Eyes shed empty tears
Unable to make amends
Entombed by my guilt

10/21/13
#622
Ink at a standstill
My muses must live outside
Stifled when indoors

#623
Sipping tap water
Listening to the crickets
Staring into space

10/22/13
#624
Without consequence
An action has no meaning
For good or evil

#625
My feet brought me here
Is there still Time to change ways
Or is my fate sealed

10/23/13
#626
Darkness in daylight
Halloween is approaching
Surrounded by night

#627
Such a pushover
I need to learn to say 'no'
Oh well, shrug and nod

10/24/13
#628
With no guarantee
This is my blind leap of faith
Stay true to the Way

#629
Faces in the mist
Restless spirits of the dead
Walking phantasms

10/25/13
#630
This is nothing new
Finding peace in solitude
An island of one

10/26/13
#632
Beaten by my past
Once a person of cement
Now a wisp of wind

10/27/13
#634
It's gloomy outside
Don't become gloomy inside
Go away rain clouds

10/28/13
#636
Behind closed eyelids
Your fears will not disappear
Denial feeds them

10/29/13
#638
Not moving the pen
Lacking a morning haiku
Nothing worth sharing

10/30/13
#640
Black wings fill the sky
A hundred crows passing by
None stop to say hi

10/31/13
#642
Happy Halloween
The spirits will walk tonight
A trick or a treat

#631
Graveyard of flowers
Brown tombstones of a green past
Awaiting the Spring

#633
Emotions like tar
Grabbing hold, not letting go
Pulling you deeper

#635
To make no mistakes
Is to live a boring life
Always standing still

#637
Down the road called Truth
You may not like what you find
Darkness fore and aft

#639
The rules of the game
Still too young to understand
Too old to restart

#641
Chilly gust of wind
Shivering in the sunlight
Cannot move my toes

#643
Too much exercise
Down one ankle and one wrist
All left, not all right

11/1/13
#644
Crawl, walk, and then run
Obey natural order
Or just learn to fly

11/2/13
#646
Love my fellow man
Is that what I need to learn?
Thanks but no thank you

11/3/13
#648
Daylight Savings Time
Another human attempt
To control nature

11/4/13
#650
Rested for five days
Time to get back to training
No Time to slack off

11/5/13
#652
Transitional tides
Riding the currents of fate
Tired of sinking

11/6/13
#654
Sitting in the dark
The lights have not come on yet
Playing with the shadows

11/7/13
#656
The Hall of Echoes
Footstep reverberation
Sound reigns over sight

#645
Ink in place of blood
Spill it all over the page
My penance and toll [27]

#647
Fulfilling my role
Placeholders fill in the blanks
Thankless dirty job

#649
Spirits of the wind
Open my heart to changes
See with open my eyes

#651
My wrist is not healed
More sleep than pushups today
New plan tomorrow

#653
As I took a nap
My cat friend came to visit
Then she wandered off [28]

#655
A sea-saw from hell
Constantly needs a balance
Playground we call life

#657
When stuck in a rut
Developing a new plan
Alleviates stress

11/8/13
#658
The sin of hubris
Was I too late to catch it?
Only Time can tell

11/9/13
#660
A decline in form
Diction and syntax failing
Product of setting

11/10/13
#662
A test of resolve
Sadness from separation
Goes against the rules [30]

11/11/13
#664
Fortress of my mind
Brick by brick my refuge falls
Safety is a lie

11/12/13
#666
Haiku of the beast
Six hundred and sixty six
Ink instead of blood

11/13/13
#668
Old territory
Can't return to someplace new
Uncharted landscape

11/14/13
#670
The shutting of doors
Leads to new open windows
Or traps you inside

#659
Time is relative
Three hundred and thirty days
A blink of an eye

#661
A broken machine
The death of my nemesis
Goodbye floor buffer [29]

#663
Can't quite let things go
Gripping what I can't control
Not mine to decide

#665
Venus burns brightly
The love goddess is singing
The night sky aglow

#667
Technicolor sky
Purple and orange cloudburst
Paint splattered canvas

#669
Subtle distinction
I am not an optimist
I'm just a smart ass

#671
A new set of feet
The road has not yet been paved
The moon guides my steps

48

11/15/13
#672
A scary new world
Endless possibilities
Lacking clarity

#673
Yesterday a dream
Tomorrow is not promised
Today needs to count

11/16/13
#674
Virtue versus vice
Two wolves fighting each other
Fangs tearing the soul

#675
SomeTimes letting go
Is the best way to hold on
Not all is written

11/17/13
#676
Eventually
All roads will come to an end
With or without faith

#677
Act as translator?
Am I in over my head?
Let's hope for the best [31]

11/18/13
#678
Like a broken clock
Ticking away to nothing
Counting down to life

#679
Legs can be sleepy
Eyelids can become heavy
Walk on anyway

11/19/13
#680
Dreams of better Times
Rising to feel all alone
Waiting to wake up

#681
Barrier of words
Making use of my degree
Well, here goes nothing

11/20/13
#682
Someday or never
I was until I was not
More feeling than thought

#683
Like an airplane ride
Life according to Kido
Take off, flight, landing [32]

11/21/13
#684
Strangers with wisdom
Sayonara Kido-san
Thanks for the lesson

#685
Despite barriers
Learning the human heart
Words get in the way

49

11/22/13
#686
Life is deciding
The lesser of two evils
Filling in the gaps

11/23/13
#688
Staring at the rails
Always just a bit too late
The train to greatness

11/24/13
#690
They flow together
Cannot know ultimate peace
Without knowing rage

11/25/13
#692
My words are shallow
Who am I trying to fool?
Tired of this game

11/26/13
#694
When alive, they say,
"Each day above ground is good"
But how would they know?

11/27/13
#696
Right and wrong: a Joke
Morality must be taught
Not a human trait

11/28/13
#698
Faith in human kind?
Can't say that I would go that far
But there is some hope

#687
In terms of freedom
The Gate is still far away
So close, yet so far

#689
Those in the beyond
Please don't give up on me yet
Learning as I go

#691
For the few good ones
There are more of the bad ones
Human race stand still

#693
Like a paper plane
On a dangerous down draft
Falling to a stop

#695
Man made or from god
Inverted Egyptian eye
Picture made of cloud

#697
Make steady your mind
Back to a state of balance
Before moving on

#699
Despite circumstances
So much to be thankful for
Ungrateful to mope

11/29/13
#700
Rather than regret
The words that have gone unsaid,
Don't let fear stop you

#701
Dreaming of the rain
Let the thirsty earth drink up
Warm in a cold cell

11/30/13
#702
Ignore the chaos
Find a way to rise above
Do not be consumed

#703
Constantly changing
The Universe hates routine
Adapt and survive

12/1/13
#704
Setting daily goals
Today's goal is not too tough
Make it through the day

#705
The smell of cut grass
Though there is no grass in sight
The scent has found me

12/2/13
#706
As I grind my teeth
This task will not defeat me
But it may come close

#707
Extra puzzle piece
No place for me in this world
I must make my own

12/3/13
#708
Of all destinies
To be "normal" is the worst
Gladly not my fate

#709
Eager for what's next
Awaiting my exit date
From jail and from life

12/4/13
#710
Quest for inner peace
The Art of doing Nothing
Harder than it sounds

#711
'Noun verbs like a noun'
'Seasonal reference'
Haiku equation

12/5/13
#712
It is what it is
Throwing a temper tantrum
Will not alter things

#713
New training program
Paying for the month of rest
Strength starts as weakness

12/6/13
#714
There is such a thing
In this world of idiots
As too much freedom

12/7/13
#716
Looking for a clue
Dozens of re-read pages
Words between the lines

12/8/13
#718
A halfway checkpoint
The measurement of year
One down, one to go

12/9/13
#720
Some say it's my gift
But attention to detail
Is more of a curse

12/10/13
#722
What takes years to build
Can be destroyed in minutes
Let attachments go

12/11/13
#724
A good kind of pain
In the winter the plants may die
But come back stronger

12/12/13
#726
Wall of golden clouds
Obscures and hides the sunrise
Glowing horizon

#715
Tri-polar extremes
Depression, apathy, joy
No wonder I'm nuts

#717
On visitor's day
Straining your ears for a sound
Will the gate bell ring?

#719
Complain all you want
Cannot control the weather
Or peoples' feelings

#721
Like a long lost friend
I have felt this wind before
When Times were better

#723
To be accepted
One must first be accepting
Give and then receive

#725
The truth of weakness
Is that which makes us human
An excuse for most

#727
The fog of my breath
Sending clouds into the sky
To dance with the moon

12/13/13
#728
Lap around the sun
Complete cycle of nature
Beginning or end

#729
One good side effect
I am getting better at
Getting over things

12/14/13
#730
Serving no purpose
In need of one that needs mine
Hearts beat together

#731
Living for myself
Has always led to chaos
Learn from this and grow

12/15/13
#732
My face on the ground
Looking at the world sideways
Even when upright

#733
This is my dungeon
A hero without a quest
Is a boring tale

12/16/13
#734
Life is push and pull
Unity of opposites
No past or future

#735
A game of chances
Getting back is not certain
But moving on is

12/17/13
#736
Running out of Time
Life has already begun
Do not fall behind

#737
Too painful to think
Remnants of a broken neck
No haiku tonight

12/18/13
#738
Even in my dreams
I find myself in this place
Becoming rooted

#739
Memory quicksand
It's fine to review the past
Just don't get stuck there

12/19/13
#740
Surrounded by night
One more shadow won't change much
No sunshine today

#741
That which defines me
Is nothing more than a dream
A phantom of 'self'

12/20/13
#742
I let my guard down
Comfort was my big mistake
Harsh lesson to learn

12/21/13 [59]
#744
Call to adventure
Journey within a journey
Transform and atone

12/22/13
#746
They are not the same:
Knowing what has to be done
Knowing what to do

12/23/13
#748
To feel is to be
Feel better, then be better
Feel sad, then be sad

12/24/13
#750
Burden of success
With no more expectations
I am free to fail

12/25/13
#752
Conflicting pathways
Joining two drops of water
Seamless, without lines

12/26/13
#754
Each day I wake up
Eyes open disappointed
Not a wanted sight

#743
No more sacrifice
No more tests of loyalty
Help me or be gone

#745
When things seem darkest,
Your revelation is near.
Into the Abyss

#747
I love a challenge
But this is ridiculous
No reward in sight

#749
Sick of 'in-betweens'
It's not black, nor is it white
It's only gray space

#751
Weary traveler,
Why do you not rest your feet?
"The Road still remains."

#753
More free than before
My heart has one less tether
Happy, sad, and numb

#755
No way to escape
There is always a light on
Glaring in my face

12/27/13
#756
I have yet to fail
Though not always smooth sailing
My ship has not sunk

12/28/13
#758
Stories and legends
Distance from fact to fiction
Truth found in each line

12/29/13
#760
Do you stay or go?
All beings come from chaos
Some will never leave

12/30/13
#762
Fear of growing old
Not just old but obsolete
Day to day loathing

12/31/13
#764
Before you blink twice
Year two thousand and thirteen
Leaves with no goodbyes

1/1/14
#766
My resolution
For year two thousand fourteen:
Write better haiku

1/2/14
#768
Do not let the bad
Keep you from seeing the good
Your eyes make the choice

#757
Make my way back home
If I am not strong enough
I don't deserve to

#759
A solo journey
No light house to guide the way
Memories and lies

#761
Watch the horizon
As the year comes to an end
Clouds glow with secrets

#763
With no one to serve
All that remains is a debt
I need to repay

#765
Waiting needlessly
For a sign that will not come
No Time like right now

#767
To uproot your 'self'
Become detached from the earth
Your soul seeks water

#769
Spider webs of doubt
Being woven in my head
The fly just struggles

1/3/14
#770
Days turn into weeks
And weeks are followed by months
Falling grains of sand

1/4/14
#772
Without any thought
Letting the pen guide itself
Eliminate form

1/5/14
#774
Dreams that don't make sense
No escape even in sleep
The walls closing in

1/6/14
#776
Despite how I feel
I will overcome this day
Tomorrow will come

1/7/14
#778
Words in fading ink
Is this how the story ends
An unfinished line

1/8/14
#780
To allow for light
Darkness must also exist
But receives no praise

1/9/14
#782
Murmurs from the bricks
The walls speak as they close in
Welcoming an end

#771
At the end of this
I may not be the same "me"
I will still be me

#773
From the mountain side
Your progress is hard to see
Neither end in sight

#775
With no reception
"Hey Jude" on the radio
Came through the static [33]

#777
Stayed in bed all day
Wishing the ceiling would fall
Clean up in cell one

#779
Does the Moon mock me
Or is it a tearful eye
Goddess in the sky

#781
Miserable guard
Resentment from all around
You make your world worse [34]

#783
Perhaps if insane
My writing may get better
Can't get any worse

1/10/14
#784
A hitch in the plan
Without a sofa to chase,
How can I go mad? [35]

1/11/14
#786
One and eleven
The month and the day today
Calendar numbers

1/12/14
#788
Lacking all passion
Another listless morning
Yet I must still write

1/13/14
#790
No longer helpful
Band-Aid without adhesive
Just collecting dust

1/14/14
#792
Slight deviations
Small ripples can become waves
Timelines and shorelines

1/15/14
#794
When at your lowest
Propriety is cast off
Your true self revealed

1/16/14
#796
Send them to the winds
Even if a part of you
Have no attachments

#785
All five senses lie
The clock tells the wrong color
Stop looking at me

#787
Wearing my brain out
Controlling insanity
It cannot be done

#789
The dust bunnies
They make the floor a ballroom
Elegance aside

#791
One sided chess game
No element of surprise
Progress in reverse

#793
Ebb and flow of fate
Life and death, birth and rebirth
Tidal destiny

#795
I do not claim to
be the bearer of wisdom
Only a student

#797
Law of Irony
Versus the Laws of Physics
Thankfully mortal [36]

1/17/14
#798
As I sink lower
Demons offer me a seat
They say, "Welcome home"

1/18/14
#800
Afraid to move on
A blindfolded vision quest
Seeing with my hands

1/19/14
#802
Each day is a war
Make pleasant your discomfort
Take the advantage

1/20/14
#804
I always falter
On the border of success
My biggest hurdle

1/21/14
#806
To stare at the sun
Or live your life in darkness
Both will make you blind

1/22/14
#808
Devil on my back
Fighting the monkey for space
One shoulder for each

1/23/14
#810
Worse days still to come
Will you hide or fight the beast
Outside and within

#799
As smoke fills the sky
Day four hundred passes by
Questions multiply

#801
Closer to the start
than I am to the finish.
Which start, which finish?

#803
Minutes, Days, and Months
Within the Temple of Time
Both God and Devil

#805
Need to refocus
Too easily distracted
Stray not from the Way

#807
The blink of an eye
Speed at which the world can change
Eyes can't stay open

#809
A fog descended
All that could be seen is gone
Shivers in the night

#811
All of existence
Mental claustrophobia
Inside just one thought

1/24/14
#812
Clocks are obsolete
Watching the Time flutter by
Like a brick balloon

1/25/14
#814
Words start repeating
Seeking original thought
Writing in ovals

1/26/14
#816
Like a long lost friend
Rediscovery of self
A foot in each world

1/27/14
#818
Truth will be revealed
Wisdom is a test of Time
Just as all things are

1/28/14
#820
How can one person
Be so incredibly loud
In all that he does?

1/29/14
#822
Always making tracks
Is it alright to move on?
Can't stay in one place

1/30/14
#824
From lull to torrent
Low intensity boredom
Replaces chaos

#813
The sky speaks of it
Turbulence is on the way
Prepare for a storm

#815
Falling through the ink
I lose my grip on the pen
Black and blue abyss

#817
Beware the shadows
They are moving on their own
Planning an attack

#819
Looking forward to
Leaving this place in my wake
Without looking back

#821
A big mess to clean
An old rag hung out to dry
These tattered moments

#823
Goal of a writer
Toxic Inpublication
Fate of a poet

#825
Sitting lost in thought
A cup of tea changes all
Soft winter rain-fall

1/31/14
#826
Before now, til then
A spinning compass needle
Direction unknown

2/1/14
#828
Inward and outward
Always a new enemy
Constant fight or flight

2/2/14
#830
Fate set in motion
It was too late to change course
Unescapable

2/3/14
#832
Little did he know
This would come to define him
Outcome still pending

2/4/14
#834
Flow with the season
With the rain, the ivy grows
Just try and stop it!

2/5/14
#836
Waking exhausted
Are dreams meant to torment me,
Or bring me relief?

2/6/14
#838
In a deep slumber
On the verge of waking up
My spirit still sleeps

#827
Three lined diatribe
Likely writing for no one
Still not making sense

#829
Dirty pond water
Moss, my physical makeup
My spirit: Moldy

#831
What would you believe
Urgency of departure
Torn into two minds

#833
Some treat us like beasts
Some officers remind us
We are still human

#835
Man or animal
My ears perk up like a dog's
The jingle of keys

#837
Search for your own truth
Only a fool would believe
What the News tells them

#839
As fate may have it,
"Hey, watch this!" or, "Sure I can!"
Will be my last words

2/7/14
#840
Blue sky and rain-fall
Purple sunset yesterday
Lingers in my mind

#841
An unsought message
Very often goes unseen
By distracted minds

2/8/14
#842
Losing track of days
The calendar laughs at me
Head spinning away

#843
Helping me through this
More than they will ever know
A wave of visits

2/9/14
#844
Embracing the storm
Studying the path of clouds
The ice lives within

#845
Ugly spiteful beast
This guard cannot be human
Quite unfortunate [34]

2/10/14
#846
The only way home
Is a long forgotten road
No steps to retrace

#847
Hello fellow nerd
Spent all morning discussing
Science and comics

2/11/14
#848
In the tortilla
Some of this and some of that
Jail house burrito

#849
Fisherking Syndrome
Each day closer to the spring
Recharges the soul

2/12/14
#850
Who am I today?
Caricature of myself
Better in years past

#851
Country to country
All the cities I have seen
Are so far away

2/13/14
#852
Mental conundrum
Philosophical debate
No answers, just mush

#853
Not joking this Time
Another ten months of this
I will go insane

2/14/14
#854
So much yet to fix
Still lacking the proper tool
The right perspective

2/15/14
#856
Failed as a hero
I would fail as a villain
Neither side wants me

2/16/14
#858
Just like in grade school
Stupidity rules the day
Bullies with badges

2/17/14
#860
Would never believe
Serenity on Mondays
More than the weekend

2/18/14
#862
Today is Tuesday
The food order of the week
Will arrive today

2/19/14
#864
It is now Wednesday
With luck, visitors will come
I can only hope

2/20/14
#866
Despondent Thursday
Stop letting them get to you
Must find harmony

#855
Brown extension cord
The escape that you offer
Is sometimes tempting

#857
Timelines intersect
The Present altered by Plot
Blurring the grid lines

#859
The ultimate lock
A hell of my own making
Wait for rust to win

#861
Live by your own rules
Rather than beg, go without
Material wants

#863
All that I have known
Is to be searching for "It"
But not what "It" is

#865
Do not be idle
Action within no-action
Walk and meditate [37]

#867
Stare into the Void
Commune with the Emptiness
Nothingness is Home

2/21/14
#868
Friday randomness
Venturing beyond the walls
What is this madness? 38

2/22/14
#870
Saturday again
Elliptical agenda
Path of lunacy

2/23/14
#872
No Fun-day Sunday
Now another week begins
Day of derision

2/24/14
#874
Cling not to backups
There are no second chances
Measure twice, live once

2/25/14
#876
Embracing my flaws
A new opportunity
To improve myself

2/26/14
#878
Starting at zero
Trying hard just to try hard
Ending at zero

2/27/14
#880
The clouds are swollen
The ground is very thirsty
Let it have a drink

#869
The call of blue waves
Endlessness of the ocean
Holding no grudges

#871
Laugh at irony
Or it will drown you to death
Still don't get the joke

#873
At a loss for words
My think tank is running dry
But plenty of ink

#875
Road of Righteousness
Not the Road to Being Right
Is the one to seek

#877
Hot and cold as steel
Temper yourself in the flames
Be sharp as a blade

#879
The new me is weak
For each drop of sweat I shed
I water the earth

#881
So much for the 'storm'
Because I wrote about it,
The rain stayed away

2/28/14
#882
One thing I have learned
Throughout my odd odyssey
Be open to change

3/1/14
#884
God is not fond of
Back seat drivers making plans
Let go of the wheel

3/2/14
#886
Luck wasted in youth
Would not have aged without it
Now just on my own

3/3/14
#888
A cup of weak tea
Is better than plain water
Just by a little

3/4/14
#890
No other reason
Avoid vain motivation
Improve to improve

3/5/14
#892
All are travelers
But not all will go places
Where does your map lead?

3/6/14
#894
Live to help each day
Do this by helping to live
Others, then yourself

#883
Instead of whining
My Time in captivity
Could be spent better

#885
I do silly things
I run away from myself
I always catch up

#887
Numbers with meaning
Four hundred and forty four
Almost nine months left

#889
Waterfall of sweat
Poison making its escape
Rolling down my face

#891
Stop telling yourself
That things have to get better
This is not a dream

#893
Hi Mr. Cricket
I cannot understand you
But I like your song

#895
Don't follow the blind
Tricksters come in many forms
Be always on guard

3/7/14
#896
My life is my brush
The Art of Self-Sabotage
No need for canvas

#897
Facing cold hard facts
I have become a bully
I have no excuse

3/8/14
#898
In terms of "months left"
Now into single digits
Preparation Time

#899
Like a pregnancy
In nine months I will be free
Reborn to the world

3/9/14
#900
As the lights come on
I remember the Time change
How does one change Time?

#901
Not nice at my worst
Not much nicer at my best
What happened to me?

3/10/14
#902
Cosmic Reckoning
The Universe awakens
Never went to sleep

#903
The Chaos resumes
So much for serenity
New inmates arrive

3/11/14
#904
Hundred drops of sweat
As I hold plank position
Great Time for yoga

#905
Even from inside
I can hear the crickets chirp
Welcoming the Spring

3/12/14
#906
As March marches on
Can't make it pick up the pace
Time taking its Time

#907
It has been ten years
Since I truly felt happy
Within my own skin

3/13/14
#908
Classroom of the hawk
Awaiting graduation
"And yet, no feather" [39]

#909
Spinning pretty words
Fooling others and yourself
Look in the mirror

3/14/14
#910
Upon inspection
Not such a great track record
Breaking illusions

3/15/14
#912
The passing of Time
Its connection to Wisdom
No shortcut in sight

3/16/14
#914
If I never need
This patience level again
Life will be just fine

3/17/14
#916
Unless I complain
There is nothing new to write about
Tired of whining

3/18/14
#918
Writing with no thought
Without counting, just writing
It will all work out

3/19/14
#920
Need to remember
How to be around people
People, not inmates

3/20/14
#922
Glue can't fix all things
Dreaming about broken glass
Never whole again

#911
Where is the line drawn?
I am becoming this place
It's becoming me

#913
Storm season returns
The last few months were easy
Now the chaos reigns

#915
My eyes drift upward
Forever a stargazer
Even in the day

#917
The Land of Elsewhere
To where my old self has gone
Waiting to meet up

#919
Delusional faith
As blind as the next person
Running into walls

#921
If you lose focus
Your goals may walk out the door
Without your notice

#923
Meaning of Today,
Yesterday, and Tomorrow
Won't find all answers

3/21/14
#924
Crane meditation
Balancing on one leg
As long as I can

#925
From grape juice to wine
Turning into vinegar
Process of decay

3/22/14
#926
You can only fight
One sparring match at a Time
Finish, then move on

#927
However painful
Never show your injury
Strategy, not pride

3/23/14
#928
Can't tell anymore
Where does the real me begin
Where does the lie end

#929
Sometimes I can't help
Thinking it will never be
As good as it was

3/24/14
#930
Sorrow and evils
Take on the form of a weight
Leave it at the Gate

#931
Do not fool yourself
Deluded altruism
Is not fooling me

3/25/14
#932
Promises to keep
To do what I think is right
Promises to break

#933
Live in your moment
Not in anyone else's
It is all you have

3/26/14
#934
Hard to overlook
So many rules are broken
Without consequence

#935
The wind in my beard
The breeze tells of coming rain
Time to go outside

3/27/14
#936
There is no escape
The Anti-Logic Bubble
Running out of air [40]

#937
With no alarm clock
The old me may be dormant
Will he stay that way?

3/28/14
#938
A six month-er leaves
Asshole with a heart of gold
Wait, just an asshole

3/29/14
#940
Like dogs at the pound
Men confined in small quarters
Barking just to bark

3/30/14
#942
Just skin, bones, and blood
Is there something more to find?
Where does the soul hide?

3/31/14
#944
Strength is not my strength
But with a fragmented mind,
In what do I trust?

4/1/14
#946
Will I again be
Capable of happiness
that is not fleeting

4/2/14
#948
Comfort is weakness
Shameful to cling to such things
Let go and grow strong

4/3/14
#950
Hard to imagine
One day I will pass the Gate
Focus on Today

#939
An eternal bond
Never rid of my shadow
Where I go, he goes

#941
Man is just a beast
Some dogs need to be put down
They forget themselves

#943
First bite of garlic
(Such delicious contraband)
In over a year [41]

#945
In less than nine months
I will be free from this place
SHE will be stuck here [34]

#947
It will be darker
Before the light shines again
No moon to guide me

#949
Selfishness and spite
These men are not men at all
They act like children

#951
Never pray for strength
The only way to get it
Is to be tested

68

4/4/14
#952
Flowers from last year
Re-sprouted but no blooms yet
They are sleeping late

4/5/14
#954
I will not stop you
You walk your path, I walk mine
You will not stop me

4/6/14
#956
Goodbye my old friend
The feel of a new note book
Blank pages to fill

4/7/14
#958
Cannot stay afloat
The anchor of apathy
Makes it hard to swim

4/8/14
#960
So many people
Constantly unaware of
Their own surroundings

4/9/14
#962
Deep within myself
In a fort made of cardboard
A kid is hiding

4/10/14
#964
A tainted journey
Puts too much emphasis on
The destination

#953
I killed a cockroach
I have killed two in two days
Following orders

#955
With so many roads
Paths to the past should stay closed
Easy to get lost

#957
Neither here nor there
All is just a reminder
I do not belong

#959
When this test began
I was braver at the start
Eight months still remain

#961
The fabric of dreams
Woven between truth and lies
Spider webs of doubt

#963
This is the part where
The hero of the story
Should fix his mistakes

#965
I am thankful for
All the support from people
That believe in me

4/11/14
#966
Despite the heatwave
I welcome the summer sun
One season closer

4/12/14
#968
What will the earth do
With titles given to man?
All returns to dirt

4/13/14
#970
A constant struggle
Father and son arguing
Never eye to eye

4/14/14
#972
In jail, all one does
Is continuously wait
For this or for that

4/15/14
#974
Random trivia
A game of twenty questions
To help pass the Time

4/16/14
#976
Seeking better days
Not knowing whether or not
The worst has come yet

4/17/14
#978
Time- a wicked foe
Four hundred and ninety days
Have gone by slowly

#967
Logic has taken
A vacation with no end
Class not in session

#969
I may not be right
But I will argue until
You think you are wrong

#971
A hard truth to face
I will die before I change
I can only hope

#973
I am always wrong
Even now, I am still wrong
Yet I resist change

#975
There is no "certain"
Best we have is a good guess
And hope for the best

#977
In the end, alone
The world is falling apart
And I can't save it

#979
Today's art subject
Purple flowers through the fence
Do they miss the sun?

4/18/14
#980
Speaking to myself:
A goal is not a promise
But treated as such

4/19/14
#982
To defy my fate
I would need a good reason
I stand without one

4/20/14
#984
In the land of dreams
Wishes and dark truths are shown
Awake, I fear them

4/21/14
#986
I do not return,
If my mind has been made up,
To old ideas

4/22/14
#988
Though I get no rest
There are far worse thing to be
Than the "Go To Guy"

4/23/14
#990
What would it be like
To escape from a dream world
As fake as this one

4/24/14
#992
The clean morning air
Sets the stage for a great day
Hummingbird dance off

#981
In a cell of ice
The walls and floors are frozen
Only warmth escapes

#983
Constant reminders
This is still far from over
Cannot guess the end

#985
Blurry images
My dreams stayed with me all day
Can't seem to shake them

#987
Spent all day painting
Rearranging furniture
And painting some more

#989
Progress and failure
I am still too judgmental
Need to shut my mouth

#991
All I see is red
The traffic light of my life
Just waiting for green

#993
If I stand outside
The rain cannot wash away
All that is unclean

4/25/14
#994
Foolishly blinded
I can't see the positive
Things in front of me

4/26/14
#996
No matter how long
I have been away, it feels
Like the beginning

4/27/14
#998
A moment of peace
Finding a way to focus
Ignoring chaos

4/28/14
#1000
Santa Ana winds
Blowing dead leaves through the yard
Leaves have more freedom

4/29/14
#1002
Sirens going off
A broken smoke detector
Alarming alarms

4/30/14
#1004
With stardust as ink
Author of all destiny
Written by one hand

5/1/14
#1006
These unloving walls
Harness dismal energy
The cells reek of it

#995
Calm or uncaring?
Do not confuse apathy,
With serenity

#997
Curing a symptom
Won't rid you of the disease
Always seek the source

#999
Despite what you think
Don't tell me I am alone
Lying, darker half

#1001
The Goddess of Time
That rules over this Temple
Grips me in her claws

#1003
With lights always on
Tranquility of darkness
Is soon forgotten

#1005
I found out too late
Love does not need a reason
Searching for nothing

#1007
Shouts from the drunk tank
Don't wake me up anymore
I sleep right through them

5/2/14
#1008
How can one person
Be so irresponsible,
Yet, in charge of us

5/3/14
#1010
Moral of this tale
The conclusion will tell true
For me and for you

5/4/14
#1012
Time to change things up
Trying out a new approach
At least, new for me

5/5/14
#1014
Inarticulate
Never knowing what to say
Speaking anyway

5/6/14
#1016
Wait, what is this place?
A jail or a movie set
Exit to stage left [42]

5/7/14
#1018
The sleepy inmate
Wakes only because he must
One more tally mark

5/8/14
#1020
With the fence screen gone
On display for all to see
No longer hidden

#1009
If you were to die
Do not leave dirty laundry
For others to clean

#1011
I rely on luck
Far more than is logical
Not much sense in that

#1013
Curse my clumsiness
Another pair of glasses
Claimed by gravity

#1015
A cool gentle breeze
Nature's kiss on a hot day
Changes are coming

#1017
So much confusion
I have nothing more to say
At least not tonight

#1019
Not from chores or work,
But from life in general
That makes him sleepy

#1021
Staring at the floor
Did today even happen?
I cannot be sure

5/9/14
#1022
The light is blinding
As I seek oblivion
Can't open my eyes

5/10/14
#1024
Retain the lesson
Those days are gone forever
I must let them go

5/11/14
#1026
Upon departure
Put your clothes in a trash bag
Then walk through the Gate

5/12/14
#1028
With Time running short
The Beast is learning to speak
Must tighten the chains

5/13/14
#1030
Waking to a dream
Or perhaps a new nightmare
Either way, no truth

5/14/14
#1032
New doors opening
Other remain closed and locked
Move on unattached

5/15/14
#1034
Zombies in the hall
What a strange way to wake up
This is not a dream[42]

#1023
Filling in plot holes
Dissecting my character
Time for a rewrite

#1025
As for Ways of Life
I do not know which is best
And that's for the best

#1027
One more empty bed
Not long before it is filled
Relish the quiet

#1029
Warm wind and dry skin
Staring at the moon again
Summer reveries

#1031
Pulled back into line
I forgot where my path was
Just under my feet

#1033
Re-reading old thoughts
A new day brings new meaning
Life in written form

#1035
Between here and there
Un-traversable distance
No bridge to be found

5/16/14
#1036
Kneeling as I think
Still awake after lights out
Speaking with the night

#1037
Sleeping but awake
Meditation at midnight
Showdown with the clock

5/17/14
#1038
Lack of clarity
Can sometimes be a blessing
Less evil to see

#1039
A silent heart drum
Without a beat to walk to
I stagger and fall

5/18/14
#1040
It's more important
For people to know my work
Than to know my name

#1041
Japanese inmate
A chance for me to practice
Breach the barrier [31]

5/19/14
#1042
Outside morning chill
Penetrating through the wall
Wake up shivering

#1043
Mix of hot and cold
The wind combating the sun
Seasons keep changing

5/20/14
#1044
A life of chaos
Peace was never an option
Only redemption

#1045
Floor buffer is back
My old nemesis returns
Love thine enemy [43]

5/21/14
#1046
A pathway of night
Stars mark the way to the end
Daylight is a lie

#1047
As the sun goes down
I punch the day in the face
Then attempt to sleep

5/22/14
#1048
In the fog between
Even though I cannot sleep
This is all a dream

#1049
Ink and paper meet
Once again, my pen and I
To define myself

5/23/14
#1050
The Gate is my goal
I must keep my sights on that
Pass through as myself

5/24/14
#1052
Find peace in routine
To be uprooted again
And start all over

5/25/14
#1054
Do not be so harsh
None are given a guidebook
Life tests all of us

5/26/14
#1056
When I was younger
I stupidly asked for strength
Strength has to be earned

5/27/14
#1058
The Tragic Kingdom
Sitting on my milk crate throne
Water flavored tea

5/28/14
#1060
Just a state of mind
Can't keep using the word "free"
Freedom is a lie

5/29/14
#1062
Denying the truth
That I want more for myself
Than I have right now

#1051
Nice surprise today
Two faces from long ago
Sunlight through the clouds

#1053
Never rely on
Anything other than that
Which exists right now

#1055
Learning new lessons
Do not give up on people
They are learning too

#1057
Thank you Universe
For giving me a hurdle
To make me stronger

#1059
"Soon" is just a word
It really has no meaning
See you again soon

#1061
With nowhere to go
Like being kicked in the head
Living in a daze

#1063
Broken protector
How can I save anyone
If I need saving

5/30/14
#1064
Far from the dojo
But never far from training
Still raising the bar

#1065
Echo of the world
Sound of life made by spinning
Circles in circles

5/31/14
#1066
Foolish endeavors
Escape from the A.L.B.
Yet another dream [40]

#1067
Middle of the day
Took a cat nap with a cat
Lying in the sun

6/1/14
#1068
Mind stuck in the past
Thinking back to when June meant
Summer vacation

#1069
The first day of June
As far as I am concerned
Won't end quick enough

6/2/14
#1070
Fighting illusions
Giving up what I don't have
Control over life

#1071
The melting iceberg
Liquid is just the next step
All things must transform

6/3/14
#1072
Waxing and buffing
Another layer of wax
And buffing again

#1073
The show continues
Yet another interview
Global infamy [44]

6/4/14
#1074
The bird keep singing
Whether it's happy or sad
Life full of music

#1075
The screaming voices
in my head, never give up
Past and future me

6/5/14
#1076
As solid as smoke
The presence of my shadow
Proves I still exist

#1077
The power of truth
Believes not in barriers
Truth overcomes all

6/6/14
#1078
Three quarters complete
Now entering the home stretch
With no home in sight

6/7/14
#1080
Lying to you all
Sad songs on the radio
Say things I can't say

6/8/14
#1082
If you have a pen
There is not a thing more sad
Than an empty page

6/9/14
#1084
When given a choice
The path that water travels
Only goes one way

6/10/14
#1086
An honest insult
Is more useful and sweeter
Than false flattery

6/11/14
#1088
On the frozen lake
I can feel the ice breaking
Relief beneath me

6/12/14
#1090
There are no dead ends
Only puzzles with answers
That need to be found

#1079
Do not blame others
If you use a clean canvas
All mistakes are yours

#1081
All of those times that
I thought I could prove them wrong
I was mistaken

#1083
Life without regret
A tiger without his stripes
Some things don't make sense

#1085
A good intention
Does not quite justify a
course of bad action

#1087
Floor buffing art form
Wax sprayed into a dead tree
Clear on black background

#1089
The beast within me
Almost broke free of his chains
Rage level rising

#1091
Back to folding cranes
Floating wishes, paper wings
Flying far from here

6/13/14
#1092
Two green eyes watching
My distorted reflection
Never stops staring

#1093
About facing death:
It does not always kill you
Even if it should

6/14/14
#1094
Not right for the job
I put being "me" on hold
To be someone else

#1095
Horrible people
Must have been good at one point
Can they not go back

6/15/14
#1096
A sail without wind
I did not heed my own words
The world got to me

#1097
Counting days again
Five hundred and fifty days
Numbers with meaning

6/16/14
#1098
Ghosts waiting for me
Some with cold, gripping talons
Some with open arms

#1099
Do not forget your
Original intention
Wise words from sensei

6/17/14
#1100
A waking nightmare
Though slightly less than lucid
Nightmare all the same

#1101
Regrets, hopes, and dreams
Right _now_ is the only Time
that really matters

6/18/14
#1102
An insane person
Cannot self-diagnose their
Own insanity

#1103
Preparing dinner
Another serving of slop
Taste is forgotten

6/19/14
#1104
A long Time coming
Cannot find motivation
To care anymore

#1105
Back into the cage
Another pointless lockdown
The locks know my name

6/20/14
#1106
I will rot away
Until I can be of use
To someone again

6/21/14
#1108
Becoming more lost
I know the path is nearby
But still can't find it

6/22/14
#1110
One cloud fades away
Another takes up its place
Only the sky stays

6/23/14
#1112
Nothing more to add
My well of wisdom is dry
Just filling pages

6/24/14
#1114
My mind slips away
These walls have become my home
Can't take off the mask

6/25/14
#1116
Sunrise illusion
A journey of 80 weeks
All just a number

6/26/14
#1118
Regardless of size
Splashes turn into ripples
All goes smooth again

#1107
Too many questions
If answers are what I need
I am in trouble

#1109
Poems with no soul
For what reason do I write?
They all sound the same

#1111
Unstoppable force
Even the strongest of stones
Get worn down by Time

#1113
Faith melting away
Which one will walk through the Gate
Me or my shadow

#1115
Sick of sudoku
Sick of the crossword puzzles
Time to work on 'now'

#1117
Sunset deception
Though the world may be spinning
This place just stands still

#1119
How long it will take
To get my Outworld legs back
Once I pass the Gate?

6/27/14
#1120
For now, survival
Sink down deep inside myself
Resurface later

#1121
Their light is blinding
Leaving halos in my eyes
What is worth seeing?

6/28/14
#1122
Thoughts are no ally
Your mind plays games with you here
Games with no prizes

#1123
Another riddle
Don't let the lies deter you
Don't believe your own

6/29/14
#1124
If I don't give up
Fuji is not the only
Summit I will reach

#1125
Once the change is made
Coffee can never return
To beans or water

6/30/14
#1126
The mindless drone wakes
He prepares the breakfast trays
Same thing at lunch Time

#1127
Not sure anymore
I think I was once nicer
Now I'm just a jerk

7/1/14
#1128
I will find my way
Just as I have always done
With mistakes and luck

#1129
Tedious friendship
A bridge soaked in gasoline
Destined to be burned

7/2/14
#1130
Repetitive curse
Just a little too early
Or a lot too late

#1131
With enough patience
Your eyes become accustomed
To even pitch black

7/3/14
#1132
Test of endurance
I have been here longer than
Some of the jailers

#1133
It was that moment
Staring into the freezer
I knew I must die

7/4/14
#1134
Independence Day
Example of irony
While sitting in jail

7/5/14
#1136
A monthly haiku
About how much Time is left
Lets me believe it

7/6/14
#1138
Though able to fly
Birds will always need to land
What does this teach us?

7/7/14
#1140
Let the ember blaze
Burn bright before you go out
Leave not even ash

7/8/14
#1142
Void of all manners
Teeth flossing at the table
You are disgusting

7/9/14
#1144
Do not fool yourself
No return to perfection
It was all a dream

7/10/14
#1146
Conflict of forces
Programmed by propriety
Corrupted by life

#1135
They think I don't know
That they are laughing at me
The joke is on them

#1137
Going in reverse
One hundred and fifty days
Time to go forward

#1139
Too much idle Time
Same amount of active Time
Stop hesitating

#1141
Glitch in the system
Impending reality
Simulation end

#1143
Can't believe I'm still
writing another haiku?
Well, neither can I

#1145
Do not worry if
The morning haiku is crap
Better ones will come

#1147
Cannot remember
Too lazy to look behind
Words go unwritten

7/11/14
#1148
Bond of circumstance
Faces I hope to forget
These are not allies

#1149
Pacing like a beast
Knowing each inch of my cage
Just counting heartbeats

7/12/14
#1150
The next one I write
She said would be amazing
Such blind faith in me

#1151
I don't want to be
The next mistake you learn from
But that is my role

7/13/14
#1152
Something to dream of
Just a break from the nightmares
Not asking a lot

#1153
Looking at fragments
Broken beyond all repair
No glue strong enough

7/14/14
#1154
Picture what you want
And stop making excuses
Find what's important

#1155
What are beaches like
On far, far away planets
Lonely and lovely

7/15/14
#1156
Writing more and more
I become more critical
Never good enough

#1157
Best and worst critic
The eyes that see these poems
The hand that writes them

7/16/14
#1158
Looking straight ahead
I cannot keep my footing
The ground slips away

#1159
Though human nature
The reward should not alter
Your motivation

7/17/14
#1160
A disturbing dream
Not so much; scary visions
I just miss Outworld

#1161
A dizzy journey
The spiral within spirals
The ends never meet

7/18/14
#1162
Things don't quite work out
Just how you expect them to
And that really sucks

7/19/14
#1164
With the end so near
Time continues to slow down
Calendars hate me

7/20/14
#1166
How to move forward:
Try to rebuild from the past
Then find your bearings

7/21/14
#1168
At first, a nice guy
Instead of my release date
I count down to his

7/22/14
#1170
Am I still dreaming
Something about this feels fake
The air is too thick

7/23/14
#1172
Through the small window
The bearded man stares at me
Not sure who he is

7/24/14
#1174
Two questions each day:
What do you really want most?
How can you get it?

#1163
Echoes of footsteps
Calling inmates for visits
None for me today

#1165
So many sad words
What happened to my poems
Wrong kind of shivers

#1167
Nearly nonstop leak
Water dripping from the roof
Puddles form, then dry

#1169
Staring at the screen
Hoping to see something new
This day a re-run

#1171
Hearing crappy news
I can do nothing about
Sadness in my heart

#1173
Simply surviving
In hopes of discovering
My purpose in life

#1175
Writing from the soul
Life and destruction is found
A pen-stroke apart

7/25/14
#1176
Other than my name
Nowhere near the same person
From four years ago

#1177
The art of breathing
The basics innate to all
Masterpiece to few

7/26/14
#1178
Lucky is the fool
That is not even aware
Of his foolishness

#1179
Jackasses surround
The King of all Jackasses
A man they call Mike

7/27/14
#1180
Look at it this way
Another fun adventure
Waiting to be found

#1181
Pensive tea drinker
With a pen ready in hand
No words find the page

7/28/14
#1182
Being woken up
In the middle of the night
To mop up urine

#1183
I say "goodnight" to
The sun heading to Mika
She says "*ohayou*" [45]

7/29/14
#1184
Surprise of kindness
The taste of a strawberry
Taste buds feel alive [41]

#1185
Fortune favors fools
The witty are on their own
Thinking and sulking

7/30/14
#1186
Still marking the days
Five away from six hundred
Eighteen weeks to go

#1187
One must be broken
To become unbreakable
Many, many Times

7/31/14
#1188
A new battlefield
Through the Gates, Outworld awaits
An odd form of war

#1189
Reading in the heat
A book about *zen* and *haiku*
Last day of July

8/1/14
#1190
A life of running
Running to and running from
Strong legs never rest

8/2/14
#1192
I wish for the wind
My body remains as earth
Mind stubborn as stone

8/3/14
#1194
Lose words and labels
Just let things be as they are
Perfect in themselves

8/4/14
#1196
A meal of despair
Twenty months swallowing rage
Drinking loneliness

8/5/14
#1198
All day yesterday
The Universe was with me
It still is today

8/6/14
#1200
A matter of choice
Seeing both sides of the coin
Choosing heads or tails

8/7/14
#1202
The need to belong
May just be an illusion
Shatter illusions

#1191
Think not of the lock
This will end where it began
All doors have hinges

#1193
A flawed strategy
Abandon hope and reason
To discover them

#1195
To evolve or die?
Not knowing what is at stake
Salvation or doom

#1197
Field-trip to Outworld
From pause, straight to fast forward
Four months to freedom [46]

#1199
Discipline aside
Take what the Universe gives
Don't reject a gift

#1201
A beast or a man
Live in shame, die with honor
Flesh, ashes, and dirt

#1203
If I have to live
Then I want to feel alive
Dead in my own skin

8/8/14
#1204
Pity the person
That knows no woes until jail
They live a false life

8/9/14
#1206
And suddenly: birds
Yellow for when there is sun
Grey to match the sky

8/10/14
#1208
Whether blue or grey
Cannot remember the sky
Was it even there?

8/11/14
#1210
My own wet footprints
I have been here already
Nothing new to see

8/12/14
#1212
Grey, overcast view
Many possibilities
Add your own colors

8/13/14
#1214
I was insecure
Way back when I was awesome
Now what chance is there?

8/14/14
#1216
Leaves don't float upstream
Overthinking overthought
Stop fighting the flow

#1205
All gifts are curses
Treading water in the air
All curses are gifts

#1207
Heat waves from the ground
Drops of sweat evaporate
Still summer, not fall

#1209
Only two options:
Try and possibly fail, or
Don't try, fail for sure

#1211
Puddle reflection
Reading my life in reverse
The sky on the ground

#1213
So many faces
All happy despite this place
Two new visitors

#1215
Thoughts lost to the wind
I forgot to write them down
A storm of insight

#1217
Without a challenge
Setting a goal is pointless
Defy your limits

8/15/14
#1218
Outworld is outside
The Temple of Time, inside
Heart and mind a bridge

8/16/14
#1220
"Perfect as I am"
Whenever I need to laugh
That is what I say

8/17/14
#1222
Cannot go to sleep
This new guy may be crazy
Not in a fun way

8/18/14
#1224
Seeking Fortuna
Fearing the turn of her wheel
Fall follows summer

8/19/14
#1226
Similar and not
Travelers at a crossroads
One goes left, one right

8/20/14
#1228
Waiting for nature
To hopefully speak to me
Maybe still asleep

8/21/14
#1230
The unknown aside
Perpetual state of fear
Each day a decade

#1219
Wall of Apathy
Wall of Insecurity
Outworld obstacles

#1221
Don't feel like writing
Today, the apathy wins
Just a waste of ink

#1223
Farewell Fuzzynuts
No one could find a rodent
More noble than you [47]

#1225
A complaining voice
The buzzing of little wings
Gnats and fools alike

#1227
Jailhouse burrito
"This and that" filled tortillas
Unhealthy but good [48]

#1229
Hard to overcome
Stigma of the uniform
The color orange

#1231
The Time was just right
And the Universe was ripe
All other things wrong

8/22/14
#1232
Little else to say
Four years ago on this day
Beauty went away

#1233
No happy ending
Beauty gone, the Beast remains
Not a fairytale

8/23/14
#1234
Purpose and meaning
Masochistic addiction
Consumed by the search

#1235
The state of the world
Is not for me to ponder
So why can't I stop

8/24/14
#1236
Duration of Time
Reaching and passing landmarks
One less day to count

#1237
There comes a moment
When things just do not matter
The truth or mistakes

8/25/14
#1238
Ninety-nine days left
Into the double digits
Last leg of the race

#1239
Hiding from the sun
The wind makes my skin tingle
Goosebumps in the shade

8/26/14
#1240
Do not buy into
The momentary quiet
Lights will be on soon

#1241
A master planner
Hates uncertainty the most
The only constant

8/27/14
#1242
Quirky character
Evenly peeled banana
New form of balance

#1243
You cannot force plot
All things have their own ending
Just write what happens

8/28/14
#1244
Anchored wanderer
Fighting against his nature
Never just being

#1245
Words keep spilling out
Inspiration explosion
Another haiku

8/29/14
#1246
Sense of belonging
Ever changing as the wind
At home out of place

8/30/14
#1248
Invisible line
Not imaginary walls
Safe inside your mind

8/31/14
#1250
The concept of God
Very much like a sunrise
Based on vantage point

9/1/14
#1252
Drunken tears and sobs
It has been a long Time since
A screamer like that [49]

9/2/14
#1254
Black feather skyline
Solemn gathering of crows
Encoded message

9/3/14
#1256
The race continues
Twenty one months completed
The Way underfoot

9/4/14
#1258
Returning to night
Looking for a brighter dawn
A thing of the past

#1247
No North to guide me
A spinning compass needle
Who needs directions

#1249
Deeper insight shows
Your mind is the danger zone
Never an escape

#1251
In a world so large
Funny how people cross paths
Universal signs

#1253
Intangible dream
My house is in disorder
Awaiting Winter

#1255
Omens of the storm
In clear skies, prepare for rain
But bask in the sun

#1257
Writing is sacred
Therefore, my greatest sin is
Wasting all this ink

#1259
Enjoy it for now
The quiet never lasts long
Here comes the circus

9/5/14
#1260
Laid bare in the light
Darkness hides imperfections
Pathway of shadows

9/6/14
#1262
Unknown to myself
Seeing weakness in others
Undiscovered strength

9/7/14
#1264
A muse in hiding
Not yet wanting to be found
Still writing in vain

9/8/14
#1266
Then the fear sets in
For what is this training me?
What abysmal task?

9/9/14
#1268
Best days of my life
Nothing can last forever
Already long gone

9/10/14
#1270
Sometimes I hate dreams
Waking up just reminds me
That I am still here

9/11/14
#1272
Stubborn survival
My spirit is defeated
But still won't give up

#1261
A world of surnames
My first name had to be earned
And all that implies

#1263
Stop and ask yourself,
"Is what I'm about to do,
a sensible thing?"

#1265
Transcend the metal
Cement cannot trap the mind
Flesh is an anchor

#1267
Though black for six months
Now returning to normal
Big toe on left foot [50]

#1269
Tying up loose ends
Will need to happen before
I can move forward

#1271
The end of my peace
Oh you fickle floor buffer
Why don't you explode? [51]

#1273
With visitors, fast
But without visitors, slow
One to three o'clock

9/12/14
#1274
Stuck in a fate-spin
Lacking a counter-balance
All is lopsided

9/13/14
#1276
The mind never rests
Eyes heavy from lack of sleep
Always on alert

9/14/14
#1278
Suffocating air
A humid slap in the face
Wet from just standing

9/15/14
#1280
Though trying to help
Unsolicited advice
Not always wanted

9/16/14
#1282
When the ink dries up
Or my heart within me stops
Then my story ends

9/17/14
#1284
Before they wake up
The early morning quiet
Never lasts for long

9/18/14
#1286
Safety is not a gift
Safety is only a crutch
Cage is still a cage

#1275
Faith and days shrinking
Eighty one and a wake up
Tomorrow eighty

#1277
Eccentric? Maybe.
Idiosyncratic? Sure.
Fucking crazy? Yes

#1279
My return draws near
Break the obsession with Time
Soon, day-counting ends

#1281
Past or future self
Is that you calling my name?
Distracted by life

#1283
My evolution
Into what, I cannot tell
Maybe I don't care

#1285
Cannot stop counting
Seventy-seven days left
Just eleven weeks

#1287
With the psycho gone
All breathe a sigh of relief
At least for today[52]

9/19/14
#1288
Asleep, eyes open
The 'before' and the 'after'
Dreams within a dream

#1289
Still seeking answers
That no one else can give me
They come from within

9/20/14
#1290
When in perspective
Compared to the Universe
Man is cosmic dust

#1291
The teachings of life
A thousand things and just one
Existence as dust

9/21/14
#1292
Five out of seven
Lacking respect and honor
There is still Time left

#1293
A drum with loose skin
Beat is as much as you like
It wont resonate

9/22/14
#1294
Then with the morning
Comes a completely new game
A new set of rules

#1295
Absence speaks louder
Presence only tells you half
Of who people are

9/23/14
#1296
To the edge of night
Where the sun cannot prevail
Empty of all light

#1297
Smoldering within
A flame ready to burst forth
To engulf Outworld

9/24/14
#1298
When the wind returns
It will carry me away
Too much moss growing

#1299
Watching the leaves change
Like watching a man's soul change
Subtle yet distinct

9/25/14
#1300
Is December real?
Does that month even exist?
A flight of fancy

#1301
All day on lockdown
Plenty of Time to ponder
Inside a cold daze

9/26/14
#1302
Life as a canvas
Painting a picture with words
Lacking bright colors

#1303
Stuck on the mountain
If you can change perspective
All new view to see

9/27/14
#1304
Sunrise from the street
Let out to get the paper
Remember freedom?

#1305
Joke of the Jester
Charade of the Pretender
Mask of the Liar

9/28/14
#1306
Fitting description
A tattered and torn journal
Matches the writer

#1307
A race against Time
This journal may not survive
All returns to dust

9/29/14
#1308
The price that you pay
For having a trusting heart
You hear many lies

#1309
Hidden initials
Another day of painting
Challenge accepted [53]

9/30/14
#1310
She left without me
Waiting on the other side
Until my Time comes

#1311
She is still waiting
The rudest thing you can do
Is make someone wait [54]

10/1/14
#1312
Beware the dream-state
Your mind will hold nothing back
There is no defense

#1313
A hopeless struggle
Balloons fighting their tether
The wind taunting them

10/2/14
#1314
If you do not care
Then you cannot be afraid
Who says fear is bad?

#1315
Only two days in
October is already
Moving too slowly

10/3/14
#1316
Baby hummingbirds
The first Time leaving the nest
So eager to fly

#1317
The crow laughs at me
As I do my jumping jacks
"That's not how you fly!"

10/4/14
#1318
Looking at the bars
Can you remember a Time
When this wasn't home?

#1319
Twenty-two month moon
Framed by the branches of trees
Half light cuts the night

10/5/14
#1320
Machine of routine
Wake up and serve the breakfast
Less than two months left

#1321
Change is on the wind
Not a battle I can win
Give up or give in

10/6/14
#1322
As 'Return' draws near
The straps of my mask loosen
Time for a new one

#1323
Despite what I think
Apparently I also
Deserve happiness

10/7/14
#1324
So this is the place
In which I'm able to thrive?
Yup, ready to die

#1325
Almost no progress
They say no day is a waste
It sure felt that way

10/8/14
#1326
In a small puddle
Any little bit of change
Causes large ripples

#1327
On a lake of ice
Ripples come from underneath
The frozen surface

10/9/14
#1328
'Days left' on the wall
Like a Christmas calendar
Tearing off the tabs

#1329
He can't understand
Karate is how I fly
The Way is my wind

10/10/14
#1330
The day of the Beast
Six hundred and sixty-six
Fifty four days left

10/11/14
#1332
The burden of life
Falls upon those that survive
A task with no point

10/12/14
#1334
Waking up frozen
I must get outside to thaw
And it's October

10/13/14
#1336
Never a clear path
Another bump on the road
A face full of dirt

10/14/14
#1338
The word 'end' is false
Day six hundred-seventy
Still the beginning

10/15/14
#1340
The man that knew all
Knew too much to be happy
God must be quite sad

10/16/14
#1342
Despite ugly truth
The me I was searching for…
Have I found him yet?

#1331
Point blank, Universe,
I will not do this for me
What is your offer?

#1333
To weather this storm
I must hide my true feelings
Behind a new mask

#1335
Racing through pages
Trying to hide in a book
But I read too fast [13]

#1337
What is one more wave
In an already rough sea?
Afloat but sinking [55]

#1339
What should I become?
To be free of all anchors
I can't be human

#1341
Lost along the way
The journey never taken
Found its way to me

#1343
Known for many masks
The nicknames become the man
And the man the names

10/17/14
#1344
Though funny at Times
My tale is no comedy
The truth of the stage

10/18/14
#1346
The price of my Muse
Happiness freezes the ink
Tragedy thaws it

10/19/14
#1348
One tiny pebble
Can cause one a lot of pain
If walking barefoot

10/20/14
#1350
On a long journey
Your legs are going to ache
Walk on anyway

10/21/14
#1352
Words bleed together
Running out of metaphors
Nose is running too

10/22/14
#1354
Waiting in darkness
The lights signal the day's start
A mini sunrise

10/23/14
#1356
Clocks and calendars
All they do is laugh at you
Cold hearted bastards

#1345
Balance is a lie
Good things will not cancel out
A negative one

#1347
To be defeated
Is not always a bad thing
You learn more that way

#1349
A flammable heart
Surrounded by the ocean
Can't burn forever

#1351
Loss of momentum
All things are at a standstill
Grey paint in my beard

#1353
A man cannot walk
On all of the roads he wants
He will have to choose

#1355
I have forgotten
How to have conversations
With people I like

#1357
The solar eclipse
From the puddle's perspective
Was still quite a sight

10/24/14
#1358
There are people here
I must avoid at all cost
So close to the end

10/25/14
#1360
It could be much worse
I could end up like this guy
Crazy and screaming [57]

10/26/14
#1362
Robots do not hope
Be careful what you wish for
Now a mindless drone

10/27/14
#1364
One of many tests
Owner of my destiny?
Still a long way yet

10/28/14
#1366
On an empty page
As I stare at my journal
My mind draws a blank

10/29/14
#1368
Another day of
Paint rehabilitation
One more coat of grey

10/30/14
#1370
The edge of the world
It does not serve to be told
But alone behold

#1359
No denying it
A Universal motif:
To care is to lose

#1361
With few resources
The inventive mind prospers
Not one that settles

#1363
It has been so long
Since good news last filled my ears
How do I behave?

#1365
Time for a new scene
I know these walls far too well
The metal bars too

#1367
The day gets closer
To feel human once again
And not just a beast

#1369
One less mystery
I got my release papers
Leaving on the third

#1371
It will get better
Time does not stop completely
But, what do I do now?

10/31/14
#1372
To remain unchanged
Is simply not possible
But can I change back?

11/1/14
#1374
The rain cleanses me
Washing away more than dirt
First of November

11/2/14
#1376
Logic was my god
From one temple to the next
Now I pray to Time

11/3/14
#1378
I will miss this place
Nope, that is a dirty lie
Just thirty days left

11/4/14
#1380
Finish line in sight
Inner struggle on the rise
Four weeks left to go

11/5/14
#1382
For better or worse
I leave this place a new man
History will tell

11/6/14
#1384
Human souls can rot.
In the safest Tupperware
Food can still go bad

#1373
No ghosts out tonight
My last October in jail
Happy Halloween

#1375
A bipolar sky
White clouds took my breath away
Framed by grey and blue

#1377
What is there to lose?
Relying on half a chance
Better than no chance

#1379
How I used to feel
I do not feel anymore
Good to feel at all

#1381
Though he may wander
A traveler is not lost
Until he gives up

#1383
The Aha! moment
When all of this will make sense
May never arrive

#1385
Night and day, the same
Sleeping with no trace of rest
Fading at the end

11/7/14
#1386
On the Sea of Fate
I cannot control the tides
Learning how to float

#1387
Through calm waves and storms
All I can do is maintain
The raft that is me

11/8/14
#1388
Stronger than I thought
Do I need to grow stronger?
Did I prove my worth?

#1389
A fine line exists
Between humiliation
And humility

11/9/14
#1390
Internal acid
Eating away at what makes
You a good person

#1391
The poison of rage
Contaminated my soul
Seeking antidote

11/10/14
#1392
Is it a new me?
Permanent marks on my soul
No such thing as new

#1393
My legs may give out
The moment I cross the line
Not one step before

11/11/14
#1394
A four year battle
Is soon coming to an end
Without victory

#1395
I got turned around
Deviated from the path
And can't find my way

11/12/14
#1396
Sickness of the soul
Addicted to disorder
The disease of Man

#1397
Three weeks to the day
None can withstand Time and Change
Seek not a Return

11/13/14
#1398
Heart turning to ice
Not even the rising sun
Seems to warm me up

#1399
Seven hundred days
One hundred weeks by my count
Sick of tally marks

11/14/14
#1400
Pacing in his cage
A wolf that acts like a dog
May one day be free

#1401
Without faith in plot
Literary symmetry
Happens anyway

11/15/14
#1402
Sometimes angels fall
Feathers littering the sky
Drifting to the ground

#1403
Closer than ever
Joy comes not from circumstance
Always from within

11/16/14
#1404
Right before my eyes
The dragon guarding the gate
Begins to weaken

#1405
Learning new lessons
Just in Time to be too late
Price of irony

11/17/14
#1406
When the day begins
All of yesterday is dust
All there is, is now

#1407
Heartbeat falls behind
Thought and instinct in the lead
But spirit will win

11/18/14
#1408
When you are locked up
You repress reality
Or face it head on

#1409
Once you set a course
Even in fog or rough waves
Hold tight and sail on

11/19/14
#1410
This is one end that
Leads to a new beginning
One end of many

#1411
The air of freedom
Will once again fill my lungs
Time to stretch my legs

11/20/14
#1412
Better off than most
But still lacking gratitude
What is wrong with me?

#1413
A deep look inside
Reveals not fear, but sadness
An unwanted task

11/21/14
#1414
Before lights come on
A few moments of quiet
But it never lasts

11/22/14
#1416
Hey, you with the pen
Stop feeling bad for yourself
You have work to do

11/23/14
#1418
A call never made
Saying hello to static
Lost in an echo

11/24/14
#1420
Adventures must end
Finally wrapping this up
Without the right words

11/25/14
#1422
My demons and I
Are on much better, closer terms
Than with these people

11/26/14
#1424
One week from today
I will complete my sentence
Not my punishment

11/27/14
#1426
Finding out about
Dead weight I can do without
Bittersweet ending

#1415
At times I have found
Of all karate techniques
Shaking hands works best

#1417
Like dancing shadows
Movement where there is stillness
Wavering hearts fail

#1419
What right do I have
To happiness or sadness
Some are lacking both

#1421
No words will suffice
From here, my actions alone
Will prove my resolve

#1423
If I only breathe
Mediocrity awaits
Time to start living

#1425
Awaiting the storm
The calm is an illusion
But so are the waves

#1427
Old journeys must end
For new journeys to begin
Cross over the bridge

11/28/14
#1428
Dancing on Fate's stage
Curtains of uncertainty
Not knowing my lines

#1429
We don't choose our roles
We cannot control the plot
Seek the finale

11/29/14
#1430
This shell is finished
End of an era and age
Not a Time to rest

#1431
My heart torn two ways
Both ready and not ready
A fool and his hope

11/30/14
#1432
A pathway and trap
The Gate is the Dragon's Way
Leading to Outworld

#1433
Before the Dragon
He will wield his talisman
Time: his blade and key

12/1/14
#1434
Crossing the threshold
An Old land where all is New
Ready to set out

#1435
In one place no more,
The Traveler once again
A new path awaits

12/2/14
#1436
My anchor cut free
Time to face the open sea
Destination 'Me'

#1437
The dawn approaches
Awoken from a deep sleep
Eyes open again

12/03/2014
#1438
No more counting days
No more counting syllables
The Gate is open

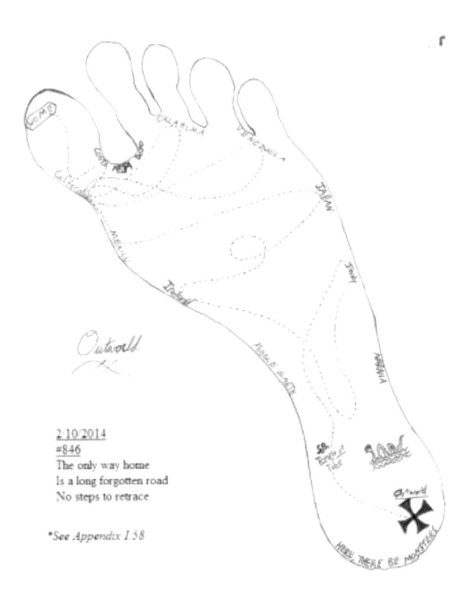

2/10/2014
#846
The only way home
Is a long forgotten road
No steps to retrace

*See Appendix 1.58

5/27/2014
#1058
The Tragic Kingdom
Sitting on my milk crate thrown
Water flavored tea

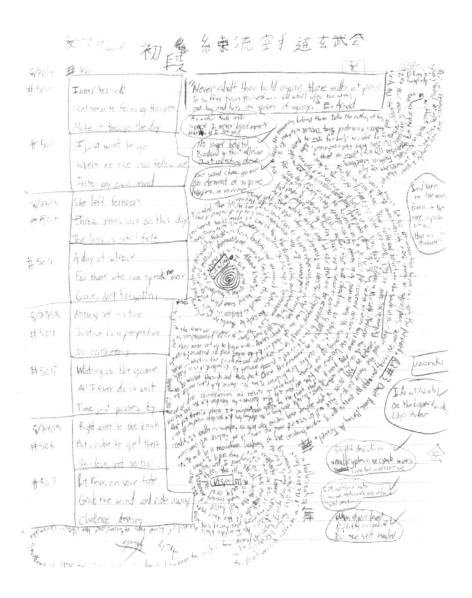

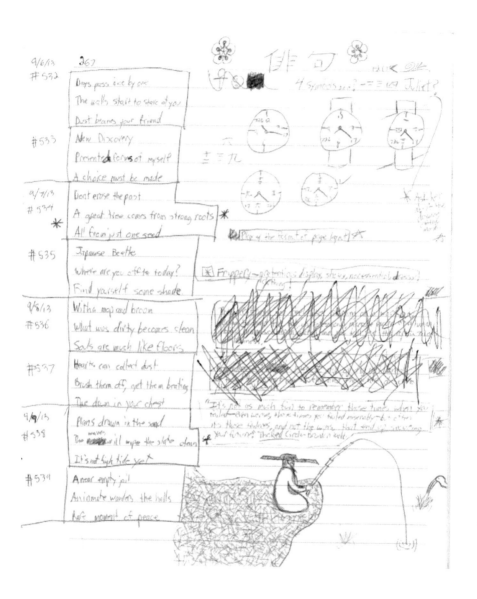

9/6/13
#532
Days pass one by one
The walls start to stare at you
Dust becomes your friend

#533
New Discovery
Presented forms of myself
A choice must be made

9/7/13
#534
Don't erase the past
A great tree comes from strong roots
All from just one seed

#535
Japanese Beetle
Where are you off to today?
Find yourself some shade.

9/8/13
#536
With a map and broom
What was dirty becomes clean
Souls are much like floors

#537
Hearts can collect dust
Brush them off, get them beating
The drum in your chest

9/9/13
#538
Plans drawn in the sand
The waves will wipe the slate clean
It's not high tide yet

#539
A near empty jail
An inmate wanders the halls
Rare moment of peace

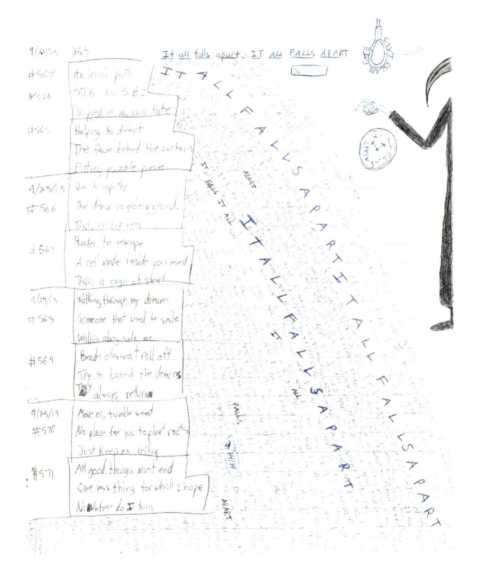

Appendix I
1. The concept of the "Four Roads" is something I accumulated and developed over Time. The word *dou* or *michi* in Japanese (道) can be translated as *road* or *way*. The five tenets of Shito-Ryu karatedo, the seven virtues of Bushido (Way of the warrior), and the 21 rules of Dokkodo (The Way of self-reliance according to and composed by Miyamoto Musashi) make up three of the Four Roads by which I aim to guide my life. I must ask readers to research these three roads on their own if they are interested in learning more. The fourth road, being six rules I developed throughout my travels, (commonly referred to by a close friend as an "odd odyssey") are as follows:
   1. Do what you've got to do.
   2. Learn to laugh at yourself.
   3. Don't panic, bring a towel. (My own personal homage to Douglas Adams, writer of The Hitchhiker's Guide to the Galaxy series) *This reflects the importance of staying calm and always being prepared.*
   4. Do not poison yourself or others. (Physically, mentally, emotionally)
   5. If you think it, ink it. (You never know when your memories will be forcefully ejected from your mind. Keep a journal and no matter how absurd the thought may be, write it down for later reference.)
   6. Walk as far as you can then take one more step.
   See also: Authors Note in the opening of the book.
2. December 21, 2012 was the supposedly declared end of the world as according to the ancient Mayans, believed by individuals that failed to do their research.
3. *Kangeiko* is cold weather training. The karate organization I am apart of trains in the Pacific Ocean on the first Sunday of every year.
4. I currently have two koi fish tattooed on my body in the shape of the yin and yang symbol. It was a shock and comfort to see the same design in the sky.
5. 空手家-*karateka*-a practitioner of karate. 家族-*kazoku*-family. Both words utilize the same symbol.
6. In the two years I was locked up I received many letters from friends, family, and loved ones. These letters arrived from many places including 17 different states (31 different cities in California) and even from foreign countries such as Italy, Ireland, France, South Korea, and Japan.
7. One of the major influences that lead me down the path of becoming a writer is a poet named Derrick Brown. (So blame him) In one of his poems that changed my life forever he wrote of a "black construction paper night" (*A Finger, Two Dots, and Me*)
8. The words, "Don't let your dreams, just be dreams" were spoken to me circa 2004 while I was sitting in the hallway of my high school during my senior year. Having just experienced my first true taste of heartbreak, a fellow member of the writing conservatory, of which I was a student, gave

me a life changing pep talk. Little did he know I would take his words to heart for the rest of my life. Alex, my friend, I thank you deeply.
9. Kaizen-改善 is the Japanese word for improvement. The way it was explained to me was that of the philosophy of *constant improvement*; trying hard to get just a little bit better each and every time.
10. The Four Roads all combined consists of 39 rules.
11. One of my favorite stories from my travels around the world was about an evening of magic spent in one of the most romantic places on earth; Venice, Italy. Through Universal intervention I met a beautiful girl named Diane briefly for a moment in Time. The fact that we ran into each other again the next day in the busy city would be what only fools could call coincidence or luck. We spent the day and evening together seeing the sights and shopping for souvenirs. A simple scavenger hunt (which turned out to be far from simple) for a particular mask occupied most of our Time. When we thought the mask could not be found and our Time together was coming to an end, the last shop before giving up held the prize. She continued on her travels and I on mine but I will never forget her smile or the moon on that night.
12. During my stay in the Temple of Time I befriended many non-humans that would venture near the fence or fly overhead. Tabi the cat, Sarah the robin, Laser Beam and Emerald the two hummingbirds, as well as Watcher, Jasper, and Jasmine the three hawks, were just some of the critters that kept me company.
13. I think that the final count was 220+ books read during my two year stay.
14. One of the very best of people that proved themselves to be nothing short of incredible and a loyal friend during my odd odyssey was Jennie. Acquaintances in high school that grew into a fierce friendship afterward, Jennie was at Times the seemingly only source of light in the darkness. It is hard to see things from a distance and I know now I had many friends and loved ones supporting me throughout my tribulations. A quick word from her would usually snap me back into survival mode.
15. Sometimes local schools, boy scouts, etc. would come and do a "tour" of the jail. This was the first occasion that it occurred and I had not yet grown a sense of humor about it. After a while I decided to have fun with it and would often act like a gorilla when the frightened/amused kids would look into my cell.
16. From the age of seven I have trained in martial arts, primarily karate. Jail, however, is not exactly the ideal place to let it be known one is a martial artist. In order to prevent my skills from deteriorating I would do chores that would put emphasis on martial abilities. Mopping would become weapon practice when no one was looking, doing dishes became drills in hand techniques, and regular activities such as brushing my teeth would become opportunities for stance practice.
17. Prior to rotting away in a jail cell, I had been court ordered to live in a drug and alcohol rehabilitation center in which I stayed a year. Once I had

been there long enough to earn the right to do yard work, I was put under the guidance of an addict in recovery named Jerry. He always seemed very busy so I was eager to be under his tutelage; believing I would finally be able to spend my Time productively. Turns out he was a master at *looking* busy as opposed to *being* busy. Almost never seen without a rake, whenever someone would approach he would start cleaning up leaves that never seemed to get thrown away. I would later coin this the *Jerry Technique*.

18. On rare occasions when the jail was empty, save for myself or one or two other inmates, in almost unfathomable generosity the guards would have left over food from Outworld and would share it with us if we had been behaving. Even horrible fast food would become a delicacy of indescribable flavor.
19. The effects of a cage can do bizarre things to a human mind and the other inmates would often react with volatile words or behavior. At one point the city police had to bring in a violent street arrestee which had created tension throughout the entire jail. A sergeant made note of my calm demeanor and he came to call this attitude my *dojo mojo*.
20. Unsurprisingly, you meet a lot of unsavory characters on the other side of the fence. Something that I found to be Universally true is that it is very difficult to hate someone that is a Beatles fan. When one of my cellmates and I couldn't find a way to relate with each other we discovered that we both loved the Beatles and finally found a common ground. Quotation "All you need is love" is from the Beatles song of the same title.
21. In the car crash that landed me in this cell, I had broken and fractured my C-1 vertebra. The best method of healing this is apparently attaching a device known as a 'halo' to your head by inserting four screws into your skull. I still have the visible scars that often lead to questions from others.
22. August 22 remains a very difficult day for me get through. I often say very little if not taking a vow of silence out of respect for the departed.
23. The elementary school I attended, which often in my youth I naively compared to a prison, had the initials S. J. B. and the jail in which I stayed had the initials S. B. J.
24. Depending on the season, if an inmate were to stand long enough in the yard, they would see hundreds of geese flying in formation over the jail. I was able to see the complete cycle of their departure and return twice.
25. There is a magical and hidden place on the campus of C.S.U.F. that is surrounded by bamboo trees. This location makes for a perfect napping place between classes.
26. Once upon a Time, I worked in the bakery of a prominent restaurant and had to serve countless slices of carrot cake. What boggled my mind was the fact that I find carrot cake abhorrent and utterly disgusting yet it was ordered by patrons repeatedly. I often use carrot cake as a metaphor for life because if everyone is given a slice of carrot cake that they find delicious, they cannot understand why I hate the taste so much. The

reference to cheese relates to a mouse running an experimental maze in search of a prize when in fact there may have never been any cheese to find. These are matters of perspective that have different meanings to me now than they did at the Time.

27. The poet Derrick Brown, once told me that the trick to writing real poetry was to spill your guts on the page. *See also, 7.*
28. As I previously mentioned, I befriended a few animals during my stay. It took me a few months in order to gain the trust of a cat that would periodically come near enough the fence that you could pet it through the gate. I named her Tabi, the Japanese word for socks, because her multicolored body offset by her white paws made it look like she was wearing socks.

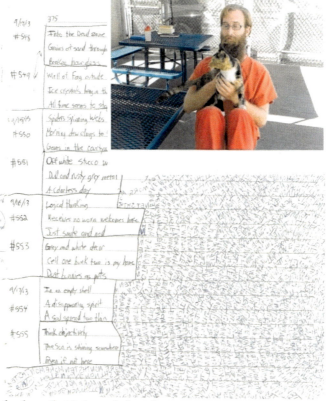

29. The only chore that I sincerely hated was waxing the floors of the jails. The chore itself was not so incredibly tedious that I loathed it but quite the contrary. I found a sense of *zen* in the repetition of the movements and the constant hum of the machine. The buffer, however, would often malfunction and stop working which would prevent me from doing an adequate job or even finishing what I had begun. (Which upon later reflection was a lesson in *zen* as well) At one point the machine finally broke down completely; which may or may not have been due to me

riding it like a rodeo bull. There was a reprieve of many months from waxing before my nemesis eventually returned. Even though it was supposedly "fixed" it wasn't long before it was out of commission once again; truthfully not possibly my fault this Time.

30. One of the rules in *Dokkodo* by Miyamoto Musashi states that one must "never be saddened by separation."
31. On more than one occasion, Japanese speaking inmates were admitted and I was asked to act as a translator. It occurs to me that I must have been absent when we covered legal terminology and jail jargon when I was getting my degree in Japanese language.
32. Kido-*san* was one of the inmates that was separated from the other inmates by a language barrier. Through broken Japanese we had many deep conversations. He explained to me that life is just like an airplane ride; consisting of a take-off, a flight, and a landing. Sometimes the flight portion experiences turbulence but you need to keep the plane up anyway.
33. One of the items an inmate could purchase in the commissary was a very low quality AM/FM radio. The major downside was that there was absolutely no reception inside the jail cells. Though I would often prefer listening to static than the constant ramblings of my cell mates. The music world was gearing up for the upcoming 50th Anniversary of the Beatles' performance on the Ed Sullivan show. Suddenly as if by divine intervention, the static broke just in Time and just long enough for the duration of "Hey Jude" to come through in my earphones.
34. There was one guard in particular that was unnecessarily surly. The inmates and other guards alike had a distaste for this person. This guard could often be heard on their cell phone arguing with people and it was very apparent that their personal life was the source of their misery; which they loved to share with everyone else. It would be unfair, however, to let this be the lasting image of this person. Towards the end of my stay she gave me very encouraging and heartfelt words. She helped me remember that we are all wanderers on a path and that none of us are given a map. It's not a guard's responsibility to be liked and I learned many important things from her for which I am extremely thankful.
35. "Arthur felt happy. He was terribly pleased that the day was for once working out so much according to plan. Only twenty minutes ago he had decided he would go mad, and now here he was already chasing a Chesterfield sofa across the fields of prehistoric Earth." -*Douglas Adams, Life, the Universe, and Everything*
36. "You alone must find the way. No one else can help you. Every way is different. And if you do lose yourself at least take solace in the absolute certainty that you will perish." - MARK Z. DANIELEWSKI, *House of Leaves*
37. "Meditate within the midst of activity." -Hakuin

38. One day the superiors at the jail had decided that they would like the carpets cleaned. They had rented a basic rug cleaning machine and after the station had been shampooed they decided to use the remaining rental Time to have their sub-station at the beach washed as well. So they loaded up the machine along with this bearded, orange-clad inmate into a squad car and gave me my first taste of Outworld in over a year.
39. I would often spend Time laying down just staring at the sky watching the three hawks I had named Watcher, Jasper, and Jasmine and try to find wisdom in their movements. I came to call this exercise "classroom of the hawk" and had hoped one day a single hawk feather would float down to me, signaling my graduation.
40. I coined the term A.L.B. (Anti-logic Bubble) to describe and paint a picture for brand new inmates when all sense and reason needed to be left at the property line.
41. There was a kind and compassionate soul to be found among the guards from Time to Time and one even passed me his left over garlic sauce from his lunch. Garlic being the main ingredient I utilize in cooking when in Outworld, it was a flavor explosion which was much appreciated. Every now and then, other tasty surprises would find their way to me.
42. For a short period of Time, the jail was commandeered by a studio crew in order to film scenes from a zombie movie. Waking up in the middle of the night to sounds of moaning and then spending the morning cleaning up stage blood was one of the more bizarre occurrences during my stay in jail. On the morning they started, one of the extras thought my costume and beard were awesome. The look on his face when I was escorted back to my cell and he realized I wasn't an actor was priceless.
43. The demonic machine returns. Refer to number 29.
44. During my stay, my existence did not go unnoticed by the outside world. I ended up doing 4 T.V. interviews, including two French and one Russian network, about the city jail program.
45. Per protocol, the guards had to inspect each letter before being delivered to an inmate. My friend Mika was living in Japan and would write me letters in Japanese which would always cause interesting reactions from the guards when they attempted to read through them. Sometimes I would say goodnight to the sunset knowing it was soon to be sunrise for her on the other side of the planet.
46. There was a community event held by the local police department and inmates were used to set up the necessary chairs and tables. Anyone driving through that particular parking lot would have seen an interesting sight of inmates dressed in orange jumpsuits arranging chairs; one of which had a beard of epic proportions.
47. One of the many animal friends I met was a ground squirrel that would often come almost close enough to pet. This very polite rodent I named Fuzzynuts was sadly found one day lifeless near the spot where I would feed him treats.

48. When people talk about how disgusting jail food is, they clearly lack creativity. Though utterly foul and quite yucky, an inventive mind can save and collect different ingredients and combine them to make alternatives.
49. Being a city jail, this facility would often house individuals arrested on the street before being transported to the county jail. Intoxicated arrestees would be held in the drunk tank until they were transferred or sobered up enough to be released. Whenever a female was arrested it meant the entire jail was on lock down and the inmates would be herded back into their cells in order to prevent any accidental contact. Sometimes the drunkies in the tank would sit quietly and wait patiently to be released. The other 99.9% of the Time, the jail would be filled with screams, cries, sobs, threats, horribly off-key singing, and all manner of noises. When a few weeks of quiet went by it was invariably shattered.
50. At one point while doing some chore asked of me, I dropped a wood pallet on my toe that left it completely black and blue. I was curious which would happen first: my toe returning to its normal color or me walking out through the gate. My toe won the race.
51. See number 29 and 43.
52. It's Time I address something. Jail is not a place you expect to meet good people. Sometimes I was pleasantly surprised to come across some decent individuals that were also stumbling along their journey similarly to myself. Other Times I would have to deal with exactly the caliber of people you would expect to meet behind bars. When this one in particular left, everyone including the guards was happy to see him go.
53. The chief of police decided he didn't like the puke green color of the walls in the police station. It then became my job, and whichever inmate was around at the Time, to paint the entire station from back to front, top to bottom. Every room, every office, and every hallway was painted a new color. The sergeant in charge of the inmates off-handedly issued a challenge that I put my initials somewhere hidden in the paint. With the right eyes and perspective a person walking through that police station can locate 13 different places where the kanji that make up my Japanese name, Maiku-舞駆 are hidden behind light fixtures or under hand rails.
54. One of my karate instructors taught me that the rudest thing one can do is to make someone wait. My father once told me that a gentleman should never make a lady wait. I know that when I die and cross over to whatever awaits on the other side, I will be greeted by Mai with a smile because I will keep my promise to her and make something of myself worthy of her friendship.
55. Around this Time I was contacted by my lawyer who informed me that my estimated exit date may be incorrect and I would need to serve an additional week behind bars. In the grand scheme of things a week is not that long compared to two years but when you have your eyes set on something so important for so long only to find out that it might not

happen, it took every ounce of strength I had left to finish strong and not have a mental breakdown.
56. On this day there was a solar eclipse. This would be the first solar eclipse I had ever witnessed and I managed to watch the event by looking into a puddle on the ground and seeing the reflection.
57. See also number 49. I already mentioned the drunk tank. Let me now tell you about the Robot. The Robot was the local transient that would get arrested as many as nine Times in one week, then go months of blissful absence, only to return and make up for lost Time. On one occasion he drunkenly refused to have his fingerprints taken because he claimed he was a robot and therefore had no fingerprints. Even from inside the jail and through the walls, his screaming could be heard the moment he was unloaded out of the squad car. When I said, "Great, the Robot is back" the nickname stuck and was used by inmates and guards alike.
58. Though my many travels have taken me to very grand, magical, and far away places, I cannot claim to have ever set foot in Middle Earth created by J.R.R. Tolkien in his fabulous <u>Lord of the Rings</u> series. Nor have I ventured to Narnia, the world created by C.S. Lewis in the wonderful <u>The Chronicles of Narna.</u>
59. I saved this appendix note for last. It focuses on the concept of the hero's journey that exists in literature; mostly mythology and epic tales. Even though my story is not one of fiction, with the right perspective it can illustrate the different steps and stages of the journey itself. Let me make one thing perfectly clear. I am not trying to paint myself as, nor make myself out to be a hero. I am merely the protagonist of my own life and have written as such.

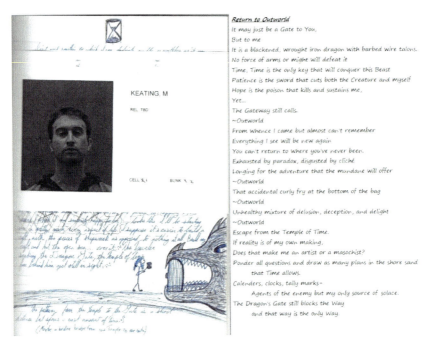

Return to Outworld

It may just be a Gate to You,
But to me
It is a blackened, wrought iron dragon with barbed wire talons.
No force of arms or might will defeat it
Time, Time is the only key that will conquer this Beast
Patience is the sword that cuts both the Creature and myself
Hope is the poison that kills and sustains me,
Yet...
The Gateway still calls.
~Outworld
From Whence I came but almost can't remember
Everything I see will be new again
You can't return to where you've never been.
Exhausted by paradox, disgusted by cliché
Longing for the adventure that the mundane will offer
~Outworld
That accidental curly fry at the bottom of the bag
~Outworld
Unhealthy mixture of delusion, deception, and delight
~Outworld
Escape from the Temple of Time.
If reality is of my own making,
Does that make me an artist or a masochist?
Ponder all questions and draw as many plans in the shore sand
    that Time allows.
Calenders, clocks, tally marks-
    Agents of the enemy but my only source of solace.
The Dragon's Gate still blocks the Way
    and that way is the only Way.

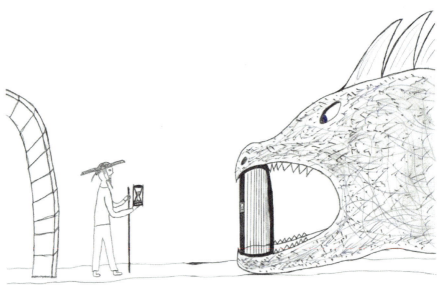

玄武会空手道

1. Be courteous in your manner
2. Have a strong sense of justice
3. Be responsible for your words and actions
4. Respect one another
5. The Way of Karate is the way of the spirit to give us courage and ambition to reach our goals as a part of our lives

緑目の龍道

1. Do what you've got to do
2. Learn to laugh at yourself
3. Don't Panic, Bring a Towel
4. Do not poison yourself or others
5. If you think it, ink it
6. Walk as far as you can, then take one more step

独行道

1. Do not go against the way of the human world that is perpetuated from generation to generation.
2. Do not seek pleasure for pleasure's sake.
3. Do not in any circumstance, depend upon a partial feeling.
4. Think lightly of yourself and deeply of the world.
5. Be detached from desire your entire life.
6. Do not regret what you have done.
7. Never be jealous of others in good or evil.
8. Never let yourself be saddened by separation.
9. Resentment and complaint are appropriate neither for yourself nor others.
10. Do not let yourself be guided by feelings of love.
11. In all things, do not have a preference.
12. Do not have any particular desire regarding your private domicile.
13. Do not pursue the taste of good food.
14. Do not possess ancient objects preserved for the future.
15. Do not act following customary beliefs.
16. Do not seek, either to collect or practice, arms beyond what is useful.
17. Do not shun death in the Way.
18. Do not seek to possess, either goods or fiefs, for your old age.
19. Respect Buddha and the gods without relying on them.
20. You can abandon your body but you must maintain your honor.
21. Never stray from the Way of Strategy.

武士道

1. Benevolence
2. Rectitude
3. Loyalty
4. Respect
5. Courage
6. Honesty
7. Honor

1. Shitoryu Karatedo
2. Midorime no Ryudo
3. Bushido
4. Dokkodo

* **On Walking the Four Roads:**

It is not possible to adhere to or follow every one of those rules every moment of every day. As the Universe itself is 'Perfect', personal perfection is an illusion and a lie, whereas - Improvement is reality and truth. To strive for perfection is to aim for an unobtainable goal but to seek improvement, even if only on small scales, is to take one step closer to Cosmic Alignment. One might ask, "If the Universe is perfect as it is, why should I seek to better myself?" The answer is that Universal Perfection is not a constant that can be measured. Therefore, the Truth as I understand it, can only be attained by reaching and then surpassing our own limitations.

火剣・舞駆

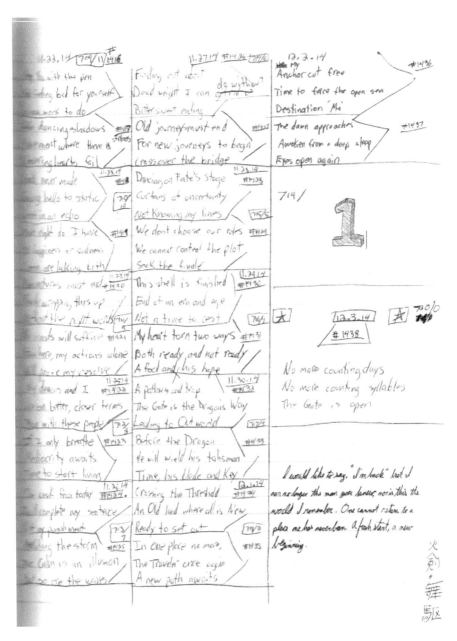

"Onward and now; his direction and speed."
~ *Tales from the Odd Odyssey of Zero*

Made in the USA
Las Vegas, NV
06 July 2022